Anatomy of a Haunting

A Journalistic Approach to Understanding the Paranormal

by Barbara Diane Holland

RoseDog❧Books

PITTSBURGH, PENNSYLVANIA 15238

RoseDog Books
585 Alpha Drive
Pittsburgh, PA 15238
Visit our website at www.rosedogbookstore.com

ISBN: 978-1-6442-6567-3
eISBN: 978-1-6442-6591-8

Table of Contents

CHAPTER ONE

The Ominous Arrival

It was a chilly night in the mid-to-latter part of 1951 when we finally reached our destination—a little spot of a place called Manchester, in Washington State, located on the shores of the Puget Sound. I was in the back seat of our car with my younger sister, and my brother was a baby in my mother's arms in the front seat. I was a mere three years of age, but I remember it well.

It was as if we were being greeted by a tour de force no less impressive than an old Vincent Price horror flick. It was a hellish sight. The night was black as soot. The wind was howling its tune along with the thunder pounding out its percussive noise as if in competition. The lightning and car headlights were the only sources of illumination available since there had been an obvious power outage. My father wrapped us each, in our turn, in a blanket and one by one carried us through the torrential rain into the house. My mother had put together a makeshift mattress made up of couch cushions in front of the fireplace where he laid us. I don't know where he found the firewood or matches, but he got a fire going, and we stayed put until morning.

It wasn't long after that—a matter of weeks, or possibly a couple months—when my mother left the house to do some shopping and my father stayed home to care for my two siblings and me. She had dutifully laid all three of us down for an early afternoon nap and had not been gone long when my father came up the stairs, scooped me up in his arms and carried me downstairs to the master bedroom. The phonograph was playing a medley of instrumentals which included "The Flying Trapeze." That music incites a feeling of dread in me to this day.

There is something unnatural, even at the age of three, about a "Daddy's" fingers and tongue exploring the anatomy between his daughter's legs. The cold wetness of "Mommy's" favorite hand cream was a companion to this hideous act. The tongue, the fingers, the cream, caused my chubby little body to stiffen; my whimpering seemed to go almost unnoticed.

"It's okay," my father reassured me, but it didn't seem that way. He was an abusive, frightening man in many ways.

This sexual deviation would play out many times in different ways throughout my childhood and early adolescence. Having to keep it a secret from my mother would cause me excruciating guilt.

When a child is sexually abused at a very young age, the child is learning that they have no control over their own bodies; nor do they have the right to say "no." They are, therefore, more vulnerable to becoming victimized by subsequent abusers, both corporeal and incorporeal.

I remember fun times at the beach located just behind our back yard and watching TV for the first time at my neighbor Brian's house. I recall our almost daily walks to and from the grocery store and post office just down the road. I remember our landlady and what a nice, grandmotherly friend she was…and I remember something sinister and unrelenting; something that gave me a frightful start to most of my days.

What Is It?

What is it I hear again?
How long will it stay?
It scares me to death,
Please make it go away!

I'm but a small child,
Only three and a half;
I need someone bigger
To intercede in my behalf.

It climbs up the stairs,
Heavy footsteps declare,
"Here I come again,
You had better beware!"

I pull the covers
Up over my head,
I don't move a muscle,
I'm filled with dread.

'Tis a miserable way
Most days to start,
When an unseen monster
Its presence imparts!

My eyes tightly shut,
The covers in place,
It would remain unseen,
I never saw its face.

Sometimes my blankets
It would yank overhead,
Scared stiff as a board,
Not a word I said!

Other times a chuckle,
Ever so vague,
Would fill my ears
And my mind pervade…

Then just as I'd think
My life would end,
It would leave my bedside,
Not a sound would attend.

But I lay there still,
Not sure of its scheme;
Was it really gone?
Was it all just a dream?

Now an old lady,
I sit and I write;
This was no dream,
But my future rife.

That's about the gist of it. I held the blankets over my head as if my life depended on it. If the blankets had been torn from my tiny, white-knuckled hands, my eyes would have remained tightly shut. Whatever it was, I did not want to see it. The very "CLOMP, CLOMP, CLOMP" of some heavy-footed intruder climbing the bare wooden stairs made my hair stand on end and rendered me paralyzed with fear. It happened in the early mornings, a little before 5:00 A.M., just after my father left for work. Foreboding became a way of life for me. Dread of my father on the human side and gasping terror of the unworldly fiend that tormented me.

There were other things that happened in that house as well. Sometimes I would hear what sounded like people laughing and talking as if at a party or get-together of some sort. My mother and grandmother heard it too. They would search the house and even check outside for the revelers on occasion to no avail. All I knew at the time, was that those noisy, boisterous people were keeping me awake at night!

Manchester has a tenacious, colorful past. It was unique in that it never had one single undertaking or industry to serve as a center point for prosperity. However, when neighboring communities took the "high road," so to speak, in their response to the consumption of alcohol, Manchester offered that commodity. With four taverns operating by the end of the 1920's, this little village had developed a colorful reputation. Perhaps that accounts for the party-like atmosphere we would hear around us from time to time…a bit of activity from days gone by.

In the school of paranormal research, this sort of activity is often referred to as a "residual haunting." In this type of haunting, there is no interaction between the living and the dead. It is believed to be a playback of past events played over and over in a specific location. Not all but some of these events may have a set day and/or time known as an anniversary imprint. Much has been said about this somewhat controversial phenomenon, and if this brief interpretation has whet your interest, is worthy of more study.

Then there were the dishes that would find their way out of the kitchen cupboards late at night, falling to the floor with a crash that would abruptly awaken the senses. That was not residual but rather a well-defined scare tactic used by a mischievous or ill-intentioned entity or energy.

When we left that house, somewhere between 1952 and 1953, it was like a dream come true! I had so wanted to leave that haunted place. My mother was very much aware of my morning experiences. She always tried to minimize them by telling me it was all just a dream…but I know she knew better, and I know our moving had as much to do with me as anything else. I had a lovely, devoted mother.

5

CHAPTER TWO

My Childhood Home

The home I would live in for the duration of my childhood years was approximately two miles from the haunted house in an area called Colchester. It was a lovely abode located on a hill overlooking the Puget Sound. We had a large front yard with mature trees, a beautiful hedge that divided our property from the neighbors on one side, and an old, dilapidated fence that divided us from our neighbors on the other side.

The primary play area was under an old willow tree on the fence side where my father put up a swing and a wooden bar. In addition to enjoying those items, this lovely tree provided us with shade on warm days where we enjoyed making mud pies and playing games. Climbing its trunk and worming our way along its larger branches was also great fun! Behind the tree was a garage, and to the side of that was a woodshop. We had a nice backyard with a fence which divided it from an orchard/garden area, and behind that was a strip of woods.

The house was comfortable and accommodated our needs. It included a medium-sized front room, formal dining room, medium-sized kitchen, and one bathroom. It had three bedrooms, one of which I shared with my sister, and a full basement.

However, happily ever after was not to be. I can describe my childhood as good times with an undercurrent of fear and its close cousin, stress. I lived stuck in survival mode. Sometimes my father would show a better side, but those times were few and far between.

The best part about moving from our Manchester house was the idea that I had moved away from the unseen evil that plagued me there. Then the craziest thing happened. I awoke very early one morning and saw a dark figure standing in my bedroom doorway. It appeared to be male and wore a top hat. The figure was dressed in Victorian garb, including a stylish overcoat, and just stood there for the longest time facing my direction.

Seeing a dark figure in the dark is interesting, because it is darker than the night. At my tender young age, this black male silhouette was just scary. He seemed so tall…as though he would need to remove his hat in order to enter the doorway; that never happened, though. I would be paralyzed by fear until he would simply disappear.

The dark Victorian man didn't come around a lot, possibly 15-20 times in total, and came haphazardly. It was so long ago, I can't recall my mental state before he would appear, nor my age when he first started showing himself, but I would guess around five or six. Between the scary nature of my father and the dark figure, I was stressed out most of the time, and sleep generally eluded me.

It seems appropriate to mention that my younger siblings were not witnesses to the things that haunted me. I don't think I mentioned the dark Victorian man to anyone. Because I felt that the move to our new home had a lot to do with me, I didn't want my parents to feel it was all for naught or be troubled by it. I don't believe this was the same entity I experienced in the Manchester house. I don't remember him ever coming any closer than the bedroom doorway, and I don't recall hearing him coming. This well-dressed entity would just appear and then disappear ever so subtly. I never saw his profile or any facial features. He remains a mystery, as does another somewhat frightening experience…

CHAPTER THREE

Phony Poltergeists

Like the Wind

Like the wind, 'tis to the sight unseen;
It comes weak or strong or in between.
To the ears, 'tis eerie and its racket displeasing;
It keeps us awake looking forward to its leaving!
It moves and misplaces trash and treasures;
Damages willfully like a cunning oppressor.
'Tis at its best when felt as a breeze,
But then messes the hair like a playful tease.
So, what is this likening of which I mention?
'Tis much the same, but from another dimension.
Out of the closet like a thief enticed;
Its antics are many...the answer, a poltergeist.

I had never heard the word "poltergeist" until I was about 10 years of age. I was in the basement of my childhood home with my cousins, and we were playing with a Ouija board.

The basement was much as one would imagine in those days. It was very functional with a washer, a makeshift clothesline for rainy days, a partially curtained-off portion with a double bed for guests, and a play area for my siblings and me. There were no windows that I can recall, leaving its illumination contingent on a few well-placed, pull chain ceiling light fixtures. The smell of dampness seemed to permeate its bare concrete walls due to a high rate of precipitation, faulty ventilation, and frequent small floods, which would occur on rainy days.

My sister, brother, and I would spend many a rainy day in that unfinished portion of our home. My father had built a free-standing, classroom-size chalkboard down there that provided hours of fun. Playing "school," where one of us would be the teacher and the other two students, was one of our favorite pastimes. We could easily transform our play area into a grocery store with the empty food receptacles, brown paper bags, and toy cash register available to us; an old toy wagon served as our shopping cart. Also, a small table and chairs were part of the furnishings for finger painting, coloring, and playing card and board games.

From my experience, the Ouija board was just another parlor game. My mother and I had enjoyed playing with it, in tandem, a few times before and after this incident; but nothing she and I experienced can compare to what my cousins and I witnessed on a warm summer afternoon in about 1958.

Some of my most pleasant childhood memories are of the times my aunt, uncle, and four cousins would travel in from Wenatchee to visit for a few days. On this particular afternoon, my sister, brother, a couple of my cousins and I, decided to play with the Ouija board; my sister transcribed the results.

We asked the usual profound, prepubescent questions: When would we marry? Who would we marry? We thought about inquiring as to when we would die but thought better of it. Then I decided to ask if it had any messages for us. One of my cousins and I placed our fingers appropriately on the planchette, and it pointed to "yes." I asked that the message be relayed to us. The first word made us grimace, "Beware..." that was a bit ominous, but we couldn't stop... "of phony..." and then the clincher, "P-O-L-T-E-R-G-E-I-S-T-S." We had no idea what that was! Remember, this was approximately 1958. The movie "Poltergeist" came out in 1982. What a strange word. We, in fact, wondered if it actually WAS a word.

After the shock wore off a little and our rosy cheeks returned to our pale faces and our eyes went back to their normal size, we all stumbled up the stairs, racing to be the first to ask our parents the obvious question. It was my sister, the scribe, who won the honor since the rest of us couldn't remember the spelling. "What is a P-O-L-T-E-R-G-E-I-S-T?" she asked. Chaos changed to silence as our parents looked at each other in wonderment. "Where did you come up with that?" one of them asked. The scribe showed them the entire phrase. My mother described poltergeists as mischievous tricksters. In my mind, I classified them along with other mythical creatures I believed in like fairies, brownies, and leprechauns. Really nothing to worry about…was it? The word "phony" was still dancing around in my head. I knew my cousin and I had not manipulated the planchette. Still, I wasn't as afraid as I was mesmerized by it all.

Later, armed with flashlights and a small lantern, a few of us were back in the basement hunkered down for the night in the partially curtained area, in the double bed. There was lots of giggling and fun, but as the night wore on, it was becoming quieter, and soon we were on our way to dreamland…or so we thought! A loud rustling sound jolted us back to reality, and then the vague sight of something moving in the air scared the beejeebies out of us! The subsequent blood curdling screams brought our parents dashing down the stairs. When the light fixtures were yanked on, the disruption was quickly identified. Somehow the furnace blower had blown a misplaced plastic tarp into the air.

So, did the dark Victorian man cause the movement of the planchette? Was the tarp our phony poltergeist? Was it all coincidental? My gut feeling was that whatever it was that moved that game piece knew in advance and predicted the ensuing event. Maybe it had caused the whole thing, or perhaps it was a good entity warning us about a potentially dangerous situation. Certainly, a plastic tarp and a furnace aren't exactly compatible bedfellows! I doubt that I'll ever know all the answers.

What I do know is that this cast of characters made an impression on me. The noisy cover-tugger, silent dark Victorian man, and phony poltergeist put in place a belief system that left room for paranormal and otherworldly conclusions for future unexplainable occurrences.

Although there was much turmoil to follow, my life wasn't void of good experiences as well. Family camping trips, winter drives to the mountains for sledding, ocean outings, numerous ferry boat rides to Seattle, and fishing in the Puget Sound all made for good memories.

A couple times, my father took me to Seattle to join him in searching through its many used book stores. We both loved reading, and I would generally return home with books of poetry, short stories, and Nancy Drew mysteries. Going on hikes and camping trips with him and enjoying frightening carnival rides together are a few of the best memories I have of my father. Although he hated the holidays, my mother made sure they were celebrated with all the niceties that go along with them. His short temper and negativity may have overshadowed much of what could have been better times, but my childhood could have been worse.

What follows is a brief rundown of my ongoing life. I think it is important because it is what gives me my perspective and will give the reader an opportunity to put this book in their own...

CHAPTER FOUR

A Brief Autobiography

One of my earliest recollections is of a fantasy of sorts I had. I don't know when it started, but it seems as though it was always there. I was a court jester who would be taken before the king where I not only entertained his majesty but would play guessing games with him. For instance, in real life, I might be buttoning my blouse (this would be around the age of four or five) and I would be asked if I would have the task completed before my mother called me for breakfast. I would guess yes or no, with no effort being put forth to bring on either outcome. For instance, moving slowly so as to make the answer "no" or very quickly to make the answer "yes." The king was very wise and would know if I cheated, so I didn't. I would receive applause when I guessed correctly, but not if I guessed incorrectly.

At some point, the games took on a more negative connotation. I would be threatened with some fairly insignificant punishment for my errors in judgment, such as I would have to deprive myself of something I might want that was available to me...like giving up a dessert or treat, or not playing with a favorite toy for the day. These games didn't take up all my time but would happen randomly more or less every day.

As I grew into my adolescence and teenage years, the king and my part in the fantasy as a court jester faded, but the games continued. The older I got, the worse the games became. I was still being threatened by something, but with dire punishments such as becoming ill or dying if I guessed wrong. In addition, I started receiving dares, like being told to open the car door while in driving mode, or to say inappropriate things. I can't remember exactly when this nonsense stopped. It was probably in my late teens, and it was a habit that was very difficult to break.

My mother made sure my siblings and I went to church and, although we grew up Episcopalian, she generally took us to the church nearest to our home. I had faith in God and never gave up on the idea that he would save me somehow.

Although I spent time with a few of the neighborhood kids and my siblings, I spent a lot of time in the orchard or the woods behind my house. That was where I would pray that the hideous parts of my life would end. More hideous than the dark Victorian man was the abuse my father wielded. However, I had another side as well.

I did poorly in school and didn't make friends easily. I was chubby and backward; an easy target for bullies. I was a bit mischievous in grade school. In the early grade school years, I would sometimes disrupt class by saying a couple words during class time in a silly voice or make a sound that wasn't easily discernible; a source of agitation for the teacher and students.

In the later grades, I enjoyed playing pranks on my unsuspecting school mates. One of my favorites was to ask my teacher for permission to use the restroom during class. While there, I would lock the stall doors from the inside and crawl under the door to exit, making it difficult for my classmates who needed relief to reach their destinations in a timely manner. I was also not above lying and cheating on school tests.

Occasionally, I would skip school. It was usually because I didn't want to face my perceived "enemies." I hated school and would fake illness whenever I could to avoid going there. I broke my leg in the sixth grade and had to be tutored. I didn't have to attend school for a good three months or longer...I didn't mind being home at all. My kid brother had entered my world just a few months before, and I was able to help my mother care for him to the extent that a bedridden twelve year old could!

Then I became a teenager. In those days, 7th grade was the beginning of what was called junior high school, and things started looking up for me socially. The biggest, most positive change in my life was that I made a new friend. Up to that point I had been pretty much a loner. The friends I thought I had always seemed to find other people they preferred to spend time with.

I found that I loved "tumbling," which is what they called gymnastics in my school. Although I was generally overlooked for team sports because of my lack of popularity and size, I did well in individual sports. I had a physical education teacher that took an interest in me, and I lost weight. Boys started noticing me, which made things seem even better on the social front. I had the stigma of being in a couple of "Special Ed" classes, but they were easy for me, and I did well.

I was slower to mature than most girls my age and started my menstrual cycle later than my friends. However, when it started, the sexual abuse stopped. There was still plenty of abuse, but not that.

Throughout the years, I had assumed my sister had been experiencing sexual abuse as well, but we had never talked about it. Our father had told us individually that we were never to speak to anyone of it, and that was enough for us to keep our mouths shut. However, one day I felt the need to ask her, and she told me the truth. I felt terrible...like I had abandoned her in some way. As the first child, I had felt the need on more than one occasion to protect my brothers and sister. I didn't know what to do. Feeling that this type of abuse might be going on with my brothers as well, I decided to do something that I had never dared do before...I confided in someone: my best friend. Although I told her not to say anything to anyone, she told her mother. Her mother told her that if I didn't share what was going on with my mother, she would.

I was beside myself. I wrote something in my diary about it, left it open in my top dresser drawer, and waited. It didn't take long. One day while putting away my clean, newly folded laundry, my mother came across it and confronted my sister and me. Her voice was shaking, and she could hardly speak. I did the answering. Her face flushed, her head dropped into her trembling hands, and it was just a matter of a few days before she spoke to my father. He denied the accusation, but she didn't believe him. She told him if he would seek clerical or psychological help, she would stay with him. It was done. He left on Mother's Day of 1964.

His parting words were to me: "Barbie, this isn't your fault." Those were the kindest words he had ever spoken to me, but they didn't change the guilt that plagued me. In fact, seeing a kinder side of him made me wonder if I had made a terrible mistake. In reality, he thought my sister was the informant. Although I helped my mother as best I could, watching her struggle to financially support myself and my siblings made me second guess my actions. As illogical as this was, the guilt was very real and continued well into my adulthood.

I can't pinpoint exactly when the dark figure stopped showing itself. I know that my father's leaving relieved a lot of stress; the difference between before he left and after was incredible. The fear and dread he had wielded in our home were gone.

I visited him many times before he left the country. It wasn't the most pleasant experience for me, but my guilt would get the best of me, and I would feel compelled to do so. The subject of incest was never brought up, and there was no inappropriate sexual behavior of any kind. Although I felt I should tell him the truth about my being the tattler, my mother had suggested I leave the matter alone.

My friend was a Latter-Day Saint, and I was baptized into The Church of Jesus Christ of Latter-Day Saints on May 21, 1966. I moved out of my childhood home and into a studio apartment in Tacoma, WA and was on my own at 19 years of age. I was very active in the "Mormon Church" at that time but did a lot of dating. There were a couple of indiscretions, but the church was the most important part of my life.

I was married in the Salt Lake LDS Temple in March of 1969. It was a difficult marriage but produced my daughter and two sons. They were my life. I also suffered through seven miscarriages.

My husband and I moved to Salt Lake City in the fall of 1970. Throughout the years, I would hear bumps in the night in all the houses we lived in. I spent most of my time stressed out over one thing or another and had many sleepless nights. My husband was a heavy sleeper and didn't take the noises I heard seriously.

Then, in the last house we lived in before leaving Salt Lake City, sometime in the year 1992, I had a couple strange experiences. The first was on a calm summer's day afternoon, and I was home alone. At that point in time, my daughter was married, my first son was on a church mission, and my second son, while still living at home, was spending the day with friends. I was looking forward to eating lunch in the comfort of my bedroom in front of the television.

As I was making myself comfortable in my arm chair, I saw the dark figure of a man leaning askew from the doorway, watching me. At my glance, he slowly tilted his body out of sight behind the wall. I sat there paralyzed with fear for what seemed to be the longest time, watching the doorway to see if he would reappear. He didn't and made not a sound. I tried to dismiss the experience, but I had seen him clear as day. He appeared as a farmhand would, clad in what seemed to be overalls. I tried to set the whole thing aside as if not addressing the problem would erase it from my life and mind.

Then, several weeks later, to the best of my recollection, sometime between 2:00 and 3:00 in the morning, I was jolted as my husband flung his arm across my chest in his sleep. As I tried to lift his arm, it seemed as though it was immovable and became heavier. Then I came to the horrific realization that this couldn't be my husband since he was out of town. Certain I was going to be raped and murdered, I tried to scream but could not utter a sound. Then it became a full body on top of me…I lie there believing I was about to die. I couldn't breathe, and I was paralyzed. Then, as I thought I had come to my end, whatever attacked me simply left. Gradually, I started to breathe again. I started to move, hesitantly at first, afraid to engage in much activity lest whatever had attacked me would do so again. Fortunately, that didn't happen. I felt that my attacker was the dark figure I had seen previously leaning out from the doorway but couldn't be sure.

My husband and I moved to Lafayette, CO in October of 1993. To say that my daughter and I are close is an understatement, and by this time, she had given birth to my first grandson, whom I enjoyed beyond measure. My oldest son had returned from his church mission and was attending college while my youngest had just departed for his two-year stint. It was with a heavy but hopeful heart that I left Utah. I was encouraged by the prospect that my daughter and family would soon follow and that my husband and I could find happiness together in this new place. I tried to think of it as an adventure, and that it was.

My marriage, although described as difficult, comprised of enough good times to keep it together. Throughout the union, my husband spent a lot of time out of town on business and a lot of time in church service. Although I felt I wanted him around more, I don't believe our union could have held together as long as it did had that been the case. Although we shared a family and our religion in common, it wasn't enough; we were two very different people, and the stress involved in getting along was significant. From the beginning to the end, divorce was a subject of discussion on many occasions.

Although my youngest son was on his mission, we were able to fly the rest of our family in for our first Colorado Christmas, and what a magical time that was! However, by January 2nd of 1994, not only were my children absent from my life again, but my husband had once again gone out of town for a couple weeks...the letdown was overwhelming. I had been depressed before, but not like this. I can best express my state of mind at that time by sharing a writing done soon after. It is as follows:

Sitting naked in a tub of warm water on a cold day in January of 1994, I began wondering why I was there or anywhere for that matter. My loneliness surrounded me like the water, the tub, my beautiful new house, and the silence...the silence that was all around me making me feel like the only human being left in an ugly, barren world where I no longer had a purpose.

The sadness and pain became so intense as to render me helpless, and I had a very real desire to break the lovely, decorative bottle filled with nothing sitting alongside the tub. It could be an instrument to my end; but the blood...how could I subject anyone to such a sight? Then I remembered the pills in the medicine chest. For years, I had managed to keep a supply of Vicodin, Percocet, or some such poison that temporarily took away my "world of care;" but they were so far away...I could barely move. How could I make it to my destination?

The water was turning cold as I contemplated my short future. Shivering, I twisted my spiritually exhausted mass of nothing to a kneeling position...that hideous posture I had found myself in so many times before. It reminded me of the ridiculous habit I used to have of praying. It never did any good, and I wasn't going to make an ass out of myself in front of that supposed higher being only to be ignored once again! Where was He when the monsters came? The unseen one, the dark figures, and noisemaker that had followed me throughout my life? As much as I prayed for it all to stop, it never did. I lived with the dread of seeing, hearing, or finding some frightening anomaly in my bed. Where was that higher being when my father was sexually molesting me? Let's see, how many times did I pray for THAT and the rest of his abuse to stop? Then as a teenager, when I saw no meaning to my life but to sexualize it, that Being gave me the Mormon Church. Not the worst thing in the world, but I gave that "Good Old Boys Club" some of the best years of my life only to finally see the folly of it all! The miscarried babies I prayed so hard to keep. I treated my womb like a fragile egg that would break if I moved too much...I lost them anyway. I still hear their tiny voices calling me. I don't know what to do for them.

I slowly raised myself to a standing position and deliberately lifted one leg and then the other out of the tub. I felt dizzy, and feeling I didn't have the strength to walk, I crawled to the vanity area and pulled myself to my feet. I was finally there. Shivering from the cold and shaking in my weakness, I opened the cabinet that held those cherished beads of magic that always made things feel better for a time...only this time for all time.

I pushed myself, pills in hand, toward the bed, fell into it limp as a wet rag, and pulled the covers around me. I woke up the next morning. It was the first time I had slept in days. I knew it was a fluke, but a little sleep can work wonders. I had wanted to save my family from myself. It seemed selfish to continue living because I knew I could no longer live the façade I had been playing into. There was something inside me that had changed. My husband and I had spoken about divorce recently, and I knew he didn't want to go that route. So I decided to live a double life, knowing full well that eventually my family would know the truth.

Once I decided to live, I could hardly comprehend the life I was contemplating. I was lonely, depressed, and looking for a way out of the hole I seemed to have dug for myself. I found a job at a hair salon as a "Girl Friday" of sorts, and my social life started looking up. However, I was still depressed, and since I had decided suicide wasn't a way out, I went to see my medical doctor about getting on an antidepressant. I cited agitation, and thoughts of suicide along with sleepless nights and throwing small temper tantrums in public as a few of my symptoms. After going off on his receptionist about having to fill out a new form, he gave me a script for a bottle of Prozac.

This is just about the worst thing a doctor can do for a patient in the throes of bipolar disease. Although neither he nor I had any idea I had this predisposition, medical doctors don't have a sense about mental health issues and should leave such decisions to those in the mental health field. However, it was ultimately the use of Prozac that led to my finding a psychiatrist and getting my long-awaited diagnosis.

After years of skepticism and study regarding the LDS Church, I had my name taken off the records of said church in August of 1995. It was not a spur of the moment decision. I was not living in a manner I believed an LDS person should and wanted to leave on my own accord rather than risk the possibility of excommunication and the embarrassment that could cause my family. There was also the fact that I was no longer a believer; I'm still not. I had lost my faith in God and ceased praying and asking Him for help as well.

I spent five years acting out in ways I could hardly comprehend. Although I was still agitated and acting out inappropriately, I had very little conscience about anything I did...including being unfaithful to my husband. I spent my nights in disbelief of what I was doing, often thinking it was all a dream, or that I was in a coma or something. It was like watching a movie...not real. Then for reasons unknown, I settled down a little. That was when I found my conscience and told my husband about the double life I had been living. We decided to stay together, and I started seeing a psychiatrist.

Aside from the usual bumps in the night, nothing paranormal happened until around 2000 after my husband and I moved into our last marital home. I started hearing sweet little voices calling "mom" again. They were clearer than ever, and I felt, as in the past, that they were of my miscarried children. Although I had heard them before, they were never this distinct. The psychiatrist I had been seeing told me they were hallucinations, and I tried to believe him.

I confided in a Buddhist friend of mine who told me they were, indeed, the voices of my lost children and that I had not acknowledged them as I should have. He told me I needed to do that and then send them on their way. I did as he told me and didn't hear from them again. I miss their sweet voices to this day.

My husband and I stayed together for another five years, and I continued to be faithful to him, but the love was gone. Then I left for Washington State to care for my ailing mother and had an affair with a high school sweetheart. He treated me so well, and it was a magical time. When I got home, the reality of my marriage hit me square in the face. I told my husband what I had done, and that was the beginning of the end of our almost 38-year marriage. I stayed in therapy, but in the end, there was just too much water under the bridge. My divorce was final January 31, 2006.

During the execution of my divorce, I was diagnosed with post-traumatic stress and bipolar 1 disorder. Because of my past experiences with dark figures, etc., and the fact that I was somewhat paranoid, I was almost diagnosed with schizophrenic tendencies as well. I was put on medication and evened out. I concluded that the things I had seen and heard in my past were all hallucinations.

Then in July of that same year, I became the owner of a beautiful new house; it was perfect: ranch style with a full, unfinished basement, master suite with sitting area, master bathroom with two sinks and a separate tub and shower. A formal dining room, two guest bedrooms, one of which was set up as an office, and a full guest bathroom. It had a spacious great room with a fireplace and vaulted ceilings, a roomy kitchen with a table area, granite countertops, and a three-car garage. It seemed ideal, and I was happy to be on my own.

I avoided stress to the extent that I could, but moving into a new house is a stress in and of itself. Getting used to family get-togethers, which soon included my ex-husband's new wife and family, was difficult but doable. I started dating an old flame, which lasted a couple years, and then went on to internet dating. I settled down a bit after finding another former guy friend. That relationship lasted about three years.

A brief description of bipolar disease and post-traumatic stress disorder follows. I feel that not addressing this mental illness, considering the content of this book, would be a lie of omission on my part. I want to be certain that any possible readers with a background in mental illness as well as those with a predisposition for or who are in the throes of this particular illness know that I have no qualms about acknowledging it. It is for the reader to decide if or how much this disorder plays into my state of mind and what transpires.

CHAPTER FIVE

Bipolar Disorder, etc.

Formerly known as manic depression, bipolar disease has been described as a brain disorder. The current thinking is that it is a neurobiological disorder that occurs in a specific part of the brain and is due to a malfunction of certain brain chemicals. As a biological disorder, it may lie dormant or be triggered by external factors such as psychological stress and social circumstances. While depression is a stand-alone diagnosis, people with bipolar depression can be thrown into the manic side of this disorder when treated with an appropriate medication for stand-alone depression. People experiencing mania can have periods of intense emotion, changes in sleep patterns and activity levels and exhibit unusual, often inappropriate behaviors. These distinct periods are called "mood episodes." Mood episodes are drastically different from the moods and behaviors that are typical for the person.

PTSD, or post-traumatic stress disorder, is a disorder characterized by failure to recover after experiencing or witnessing a terrifying event and is often considered a precursor to bipolar disorder. Need I say more? It all started in that house—the fear of my father and the unidentified anomaly that enjoyed striking fear into my very young psyche. Although I cannot recall which came first, I can say they both caused me a profound degree of stress. I have seen several mental health experts, be they psychotherapists, psychiatrists, or psychopharmacologists, who have indicated PTSD has always been the biggest obstacle in my fight for sanity. From my own perspective, my predisposition to bipolar disorder was triggered a long time ago by the PTSD and reared its ugly head in varying degrees many times before I was diagnosed in the latter part of 2005.

Chapter Six

Haunted

I had been on bipolar meds for approximately a year before I moved into my new home in July of 2006. I still heard things and fought against the mania. I used my medications as directed and saw my counselor each week with very few exceptions.

On October 4, 2008, my mother passed away. This is the saddest experience I have ever been through. My feelings are best described in the following writing I dedicated to her a few years later:

Barbara Diane Holland

From My Heart

Oh, mother of mine,
It's been such a long time;
Won't you please come back?
You wouldn't have to stay,
Well maybe just for a day.
We could watch a movie...
Or go for a walk,
And have a long talk,
Or just hold hands.
I don't mean to concern you,
Maybe you could just give me a clue
When you're somewhere nearby.
I sure hope you're happy,
And although I sound sappy,
It's just that I miss you...every day.

I've had a couple amazing dreams about my mother. I believe they were more than dreams. The first one was like a short movie to help me through my loss. It was very vivid and occurred the morning of November 11, 2008. My sister, brother, mother, and I were the cast.

Across the street from our childhood home lived some kind neighbors who would allow us to enjoy their beach now and again when we were children. They had a long, downhill driveway that led to the shore of the bay. Protruding into the water beyond the bayfront was a concrete boat launch. In the dream, my brother, sister, and I were pulling some tall weeds along the side of it and laying them atop the launch. Suddenly, the tide started coming in, and we were scurrying to remove the weeds from the launch before the waves took them out. I looked up to see my mother, who I was aware had passed on, start helping us with the task. I was awestruck. I had never seen my mother in a swimsuit or in any body of water. In life, she couldn't swim and was too self-conscious to wear a swimsuit. But there she was in a swimsuit, and I watched her as she walked to the edge of the launch. She was no longer in a crippled state as she had been in life. Standing tall, she turned away from the water, stretched her arms over her head, and started falling backward into the bay. I panicked and started to go after her. Then, my brother uttered the only words that were spoken in the dream: "Let her go, Barbie. Just let her go."

She looked like a pro as she broke into a back stroke...so graceful and unafraid she was. I was content that she would be all right, but it was all so touching, and I woke up crying. In the dream, she didn't acknowledge that we were there. She was on her own journey, and for the first time in a long time, she didn't need our help. It was such a beautiful, touching dream. Seeing my mother looking healthy and strong for the first time since my early childhood memories took my breath. She comes around now and again...I can smell her perfume, and I continue to see and visit her in my dreams.

It wasn't long after moving into my Broomfield home that I started experiencing strange happenings. I was hearing voices, knocking, tapping, and other sundry things. It didn't happen a lot, and I chalked it up to the house settling, a vivid imagination, possibly my mental condition, or side effects from the meds I was taking. However, I did call the police on a few occasions believing I had an intruder in my home. I was awakened several times to the sound of my electric toothbrush being turned on and off and other noises coming from my master bathroom. The experiences were infrequent and at a low intensity in the beginning; however, by 2010, they had become overwhelming and something that I could no longer ignore.

What follows is a journal of what I was coming to believe was a haunting. I add notes from a retrospective point of view that I think might clarify some of these odd happenings. This is the crux of my book. It is lengthy and somewhat repetitious, but real. Although some of my ideas and conclusions play out differently in the journal from what I have come to believe in the end, except for a few grammatical errors, I have left them as I wrote them. It is a journalistic approach and subsequent anatomy of my haunting. For those who study and explore this subject avidly, I hope the journal will add to their understanding. For those who have picked up this book more for its entertainment value, I have bold-typed the more interesting, less repetitious parts.

The journal is not an attempt to convince you, the reader, of anything. It is my hope that it will be entertaining, possibly broaden your perspective of this life, and give some a few unexpected aha moments. Although I have come up with my own conclusions, yours are just as valuable, and there are no fictional experiences to sway you in my direction. In fact, I have knowingly included observations that will probably do just the opposite, my intent first and foremost, to be honest. The conclusion of this book is directly related to this haunting and was not realized until I reached what I thought was its end. This will become evident, and it is my expectation that you will be as surprised and mystified by it as I am...

CHAPTER SEVEN
2010

January 15: Doorknob sound. Although this sound began with the master bedroom door, it has now extended to the laundry room and garage entry doors. It sounds as though either door is jammed or locked shut and that someone is jiggling the doorknob in an effort to open it.

January 19: Missing manicure set. It's an heirloom. It was a gift from my father to my mother. I use it a lot and couldn't find it today. It has always, until today, been in my nightstand. Also, my deodorant has disappeared.

> *Note: Classic description of poltergeists...noisy spirits, tricksters, masters of chaos and confusion, THIEVES. More information about poltergeists is included in Chapter 14.*

January 23: I Keep hearing what sounds like a creaky door opening.

February 2: I heard heavy breathing and muffled voices last night. I had an appointment with my psychotherapist today. I may need to get my meds changed.

February 7: I was talking to my sister on the landline, and suddenly the phone made a "ghhhhhhh" sound and went dead. I stepped into my office to do some checking and found the answering machine and charger portion of my landline unplugged and the receiver lying on the floor. It kind of spooked me, so I plugged it back in, called my sister back, and had her listen as I searched the house. My exterior doors were locked, and there were no intruders that I could find.

February 25: I Had my son come over to install dead bolts on the service door, basement door, and entry door from the garage into the house.

March 19: Yesterday I turned my house upside down looking for an insurance invoice...finally gave up. I later found it lying on my bed.

Later, I couldn't find my maintenance check and eventually found IT on my bed. I had gone through my bedroom on both of my hunting trips and saw neither of them. It wasn't until I gave up that I found each of them, on different occasions, on my bed. I want to blame it on someone else, but there's nobody here but me...well, I guess that's speculative. If not me, possibly that pesky roommate of mine that I refer to as a poltergeist!

July 17: At about 11:25 P.M., while sitting at my office desk, I heard a loud chomping sound like a large animal chewing on food. Shortly after, while descending the stairs to the basement, I felt as though something was behind me. As I was walking back to my office, it sounded like an item with a hard surface was wobbling on my desk, but when I entered the office, I couldn't see activity anywhere in that space. When the sound stopped, I stomped on the floor in an attempt to cause the wobbling sound again, but nothing happened. I even tried shaking the desk, but it is large and heavy and I didn't have the strength. I couldn't mimic the sound. This entire experience was very real and frightening.

> Note: *The loud chomping sound is something one would expect to hear from some sort of beastly creature. It was very disturbing, as was the feeling of something following me. I would classify this as an inhuman anomaly of some kind.*

July 20: The doorknob on the garage entry door to the house was jiggling off and on today. I have yet to see it happening. I just hear it. When I get close to the door, the sound stops. **Pillow scratching tonight.**

> *Note: I sometimes hear what sounds like scratching under my pillow at night. This has been going on since early childhood. It isn't a good sound and varies in its intensity. The scratching is underneath the pillow and generally localized under my ear while lying on my side. It happens when I'm resting or attempting to go to sleep.*

August 12: At night, in the dark, it sounds like it's raining. I get up and check, and there is no rain. I go to bed, lie down, and hear it again. This has been happening for the past few nights.

August 17: Hallucinating again…at least that's what they tell me!

> *Note: A hallucination, in its broadest sense, is a perception in the absence of a stimulus. In a stricter sense, hallucinations are defined as perceptions in a conscious and awake state in the absence of external stimuli. They have qualities of real perception in that they are vivid, substantial, and located in external, objective space. Wakefulness distinguishes hallucinations from the related phenomena of dreaming, which involves sleep; illusion, which involves distorted or misinterpreted real perception; imagery, which does not mimic real perception and is under voluntary control; and pseudohallucination, which is an involuntary experience vivid enough to be regarded as a hallucination but recognized by the individual not to be the result of external stimuli. Hallucinations also differ from "delusional perceptions," in which a correctly sensed and interpreted stimulus (i.e., a real perception) is given some additional (and typically bizarre) significance. Hallucinations can occur in any sensory modality.*

September 22: As I was getting ready for bed, I felt a cold breeze behind my legs. Light bulbs flickered in the master bathroom and bedroom, door-knobs were jiggling, and I heard knocking. I was wide awake. From my limited studies, I've learned that flickering lights and a cold, sudden breeze can be indicative of a spirit or ghost trying to manifest. The jiggling door-knobs and knocks seem like signs that someone or something wants in. However, it seems as though something has already made itself to home!

October 4: At about 1:25 P.M., while sitting in my office, I heard the front doorknob jiggle. At 1:35 P.M. I heard it again. At 1:55 P.M., I heard the door-knob jiggle on the basement door. I heard a few other quiet sounds. **Today is the anniversary of my Mother's death.**

November 21: I had a nightmare, although it seemed real. I heard the phone ring one very long ring, and then I felt pressure on top of me as I have before.

December 8: I woke up to someone knocking on the front door. I've been waking up to the phone and doorbell ringing as well. It is generally at an ungodly hour, and nobody is on the other end of the phone or at the door. I'm getting very little sleep.

December 18: Pillow scratching last night. It lasted longer than ever.

I didn't keep a record of all my experiences. These were just the ones I wrote down.

> *Note: By the latter part of 2009, things had picked up significantly, and that is when I also started noticing my light bulbs burning out more frequently. Although I realized all the ways this can be "de-bunked" as far as paranormal activity goes, I felt the need to start keeping track of the electrical disturbances going on because of the other signs that also signaled possible paranormal activity.*

CHAPTER EIGHT

2011

I didn't keep up on my journaling in 2011 as well as I wish I had but will include what I have.

January 28: Deep breathing surrounded me. Short in duration; maybe 60 seconds.

February 7: I heard the doorknob sound between 9:00–9:30 A.M. longer and louder than usual.

February 26: At approximately 9:00 A.M., I heard the VHS tapes rattling in the armoire drawer located under the television in the master bedroom. I was a little groggy when this happened, and I've heard that noise before. Still lying in bed, I felt weight coming down on me. It started out light but got heavier and heavier. I wasn't in pain but found it difficult to breathe. Then it felt as though whatever was on me was lifting its weight a little, and then like I was being given some kind of massage but on my front, not my back. The pressure increased, as did the movement. I looked at the down cover over me and saw it moving with the massage. It was frightening to see! I felt an uncomfortable tingling going on from my head to my toes...what next? Thankfully, the force left as unexpectedly as it arrived. It was an energy that had control

over me; I couldn't move or speak. I could not see the aberration performing this vile act.

April 11: I was in my master bathroom this afternoon about 1:50 applying my makeup. Neither the TV nor the radio was on. The sound I heard was so odd and out of character for my home that it stopped me dead in my tracks or, more accurately, mid-mascara application. I just stood there, mascara wand in hand, looking in the mirror wide-eyed and paralyzed with fear. It sounded like a large animal with a large tongue was just outside the door of my master bathroom lapping liquid from what had to be a very large bowl. I have no animals, and although it made no sense, these are the only words I can find to describe it. This went on for about a minute…it was very loud. I remained in my paralytic state for a minute or two after this uncomfortable sound stopped and then slowly lowered my mascara wand to the bathroom counter and tiptoed to the bathroom door. It was already partially closed, and I didn't take the time to look at what may have been beyond the doorway but quickly shut and locked it. I stayed in the bathroom for about 15 minutes after, not knowing what to do next. I finally found the courage to crack the door open and peek into my bedroom. I continued the process, opening the door a little bit at a time lest I should be attacked by a bear or a lion or God knows what else! There was nothing there, and nothing was out of place.

Note: I've seen and heard a lot of things that most people haven't, but that experience is high on my list as one of the most frightening I have ever experienced. Hallucination or not, it was very real to me. I mentioned a similar experience in my office on July 17, 2010, but on a scale of 1-10, it was about an 8. This experience didn't fit within that criteria. It was ungodly and so loud! If I were to classify this noise, I would refer to it, along with the July 17 anomaly, as inhuman.

April 15: It was about 12:00 A.M. when I retired for the night. As I was lying in bed hoping to get a good night's sleep, I noticed the room becoming darker and darker. It seemed that someone was gradually closing my bedroom door. I turned on the nightstand lamp, and the door was open. I'm not going to dwell on it.

May 16: As I was attempting to go to sleep for the night, I heard the bedroom doorknob jiggle. The door was open. I'm beginning to think this is simply an intimidation tactic…just another way to make noise.

May 22: I heard what sounded like gravel in a box being shaken this morning in my bedroom. There was about a five second break between the shakes. It sounded like it was happening behind my headboard. There is maybe a four-inch space between my headboard and the wall. Of course, it makes no sense.

Note: Poltergeist noise.

July 7: Light bulbs keep burning out…two in my master closet need replacing.

July 8: I keep hearing untimely beeps in the kitchen area. It's not a scary experience. It sounds much like a timer going off on a stove or some other appliance. When I enter the kitchen to determine its origin, it stops. As I leave the area, it starts up again. This happens a lot, so today I decided to find out how many times this activity would repeat itself. As I would step away from the kitchen, the beeping would start; I would then take a couple steps toward the kitchen, and it would stop. It was as if I was setting off a very quiet motion sensor! I repeated this exercise five times in a row, at which point the beeping stopped and I was able go in and out of the kitchen without incident.

This was not scary in any way, but rather like a game. I can't come up with any other conclusion but that there is something unseen that can manipulate or mimic the appliances and kitchen gadgets that produce beeping sounds in my kitchen. I felt nothing evil around me while performing this little experiment, quite the contrary.

Note: I believe this type of activity is brought on by the poltergeist or a ghost.

July 9: The doorbell woke me up about 4:00 A.M. I got up, checked things out, and nobody was there…not a surprise. As I've mentioned before, this sort of thing happens a lot. I simply don't write it in my journal each time.

July 19: While sitting at my desk doing paperwork in my office, I heard what seemed to be scratching in the wall between the office and dining room. It could be an animal stuck in the wall, I guess…not a pleasant sound. I'll have to mention it to my exterminator the next time he's here. He comes once a month.

Note: The sound of scratching in/on the walls, in a supernatural sense, is generally related to poltergeist or demonic activity. It feels demonic to me, and I generally hear it in the office/dining room area. It's a disturbing sound that I believe is meant to strike fear in the soul of the listener.

This being the first time I have used the term "supernatural," I need to offer some explanation for its usage. In a nutshell, paranormal refers to the concept that there are mysteries in this world we cannot yet explain…but there is potential, given the scientific strides that have been made in this area of expertise, that we may one day better understand them.

Supernatural refers to beings and concepts that will probably never be able to be explained through scientific methods. Otherworldly beings—Gods, angels, demons, etc.—are faith-based and considered to be unfathomable in the scientific world. In general, I will use the word "paranormal." When referring to things demonic, for the most part, I will use the word "supernatural." I find the word both perplexing and subjective; when in doubt, I will use the word paranormal.

October 30: I heard doorknob jiggling on my bedroom door…as usual the door is partially open.

November 7: After retiring for the night, I heard a sound like something significant dropped in the family room. As I exited my bedroom to inspect, I heard something that sounded like a small rubber ball hitting the dining room windows. I heard it twice…one hit after the other. Then I heard very distinct talking and laughing coming from downstairs. It wasn't at all scary, but as I got close to opening the basement door, it stopped. I didn't get close enough to decipher the conversation.

December 13: Doorknob jiggling sound.

December 21: I noticed today that two more light bulbs have gone out, and one of my smoke detectors is chirping.

Chapter Nine

2012

January 23: I woke up this morning at approximately 6:30 to the sound of a metronome. I don't own one or have one in my house but heard one nonetheless. It stopped, and then I heard faint knocking. It seemed to be coming from the family room, so I closed the bedroom door. Whatever makes these sounds sometimes seems compelled to make them, and at times the knocking almost sounds like it's being done in a trance-like state. A while later, I headed out of the bedroom to turn down the heat, and as I stepped into the family room, the knocking stopped. As soon as I returned to my bedroom, it started up again.

January 24: I keep losing earrings. I'll accidently drop one and never see it again.

February 12: I awakened early this morning to the sound of the doorbell… nobody at the door.

February 15: I heard three "dings" behind my headboard last night. It was much like the sound of a hotel call bell. No, I don't have a hotel call bell anywhere in this house!

March 4: Last night, as I lay in bed on my side, I felt what seemed to be someone lying behind me. Then I felt an arm wrap around me and squeeze me until I couldn't breathe, and I feared for my life. When it scared me to the point that I thought I was going to die, the presence left. The scariest part of this experience is that it felt very human.

March 28: I woke up to what sounded like a man clearing his throat. Throat clearing was broken into three times with a short pause between.

April 11: My nephew was in town, and I brought the family together for a visit. After everyone but he and my daughter left, THEY heard the doorknob jiggle on my bedroom door. Pretty sure THAT wasn't a hallucination, unless they both had the same hallucination at the same time! Surprisingly, I didn't hear it. I'm probably so accustomed to it I don't always notice.

April 28: I woke up early this morning to find myself levitated approximately 12 inches from the bed mattress. Then I felt something heavy on top of me pushing me back down. Then, as I felt my body connect with the mattress, the weight continued to push down on my body...I couldn't breathe and thought I would surely be crushed; but then whatever was on me simply wasn't anymore. I don't know why, but I felt that the anomaly on top of me was not the only one in the room.

> *Note: Upon finding myself levitated, it was as though I was stiff as a board from head to toe. I believe this sort of activity to be demonic.*

May 3: I had to replace two light bulbs in the family room. Then, as I was retiring for the night, I noticed that the light bulb in one of the bedside lamps in the master bedroom was out.

May 4: I went downstairs to the basement. I heard what sounded like two glasses clinking twice. I have a lot of glass down there. I don't know...

May 8: I purchased a digital recorder to see if I could pick up some sounds.

May 9: More of the usual sounds at night…so tired.

May 10: My house alarm went off at 2:26 A.M. I think something is trying to tell me it's real. Usual noises as well. There was no logical reason for the alarm to go off.

May 13: I entered the garage to get in the car and was startled when a board about 24"x 4" x ½" thick, which had been leaning against the wall for about two years, fell backward. That makes no sense! It was leaning against the wall with probably a four-inch space at the bottom from the wall, and it fell straight backward! Things are getting weird around here.

Later, I was coming upstairs from the basement and locked the door as usual. I heard the lock being manipulated while walking up the first three stairs. I went back and checked it, and it was still locked. **Then I heard a noise that sounded like a large piece of furniture being dragged on the basement floor. I'll check that out later.**

> *Note: The board falling backward was the first time I had even come close to seeing something manipulated to make a sound. Although my back was turned and I didn't see the board fall, all evidence and physical senses indicated that the sound came from the board being tipped over by something unseen. It seemed that this activity was timed and manipulated by something wanting to show its capacity to interact with the physical realm.*

May 15: I heard a couple clunks and a very loud whipping or whacking sound while in bed last night.

May 20: I was going to replace a light bulb, but it just needed to be turned tighter.

May 26: I was purchasing a new car from a broker who delivered it to me today. He asked for my insurance card and registration for the car I was trading in. I looked in the glove compartment where I keep them, and neither were there. I then checked my purse for an insurance card, since I keep one there as well…no such luck! I dumped the contents of my purse on the floor and rifled through it. I then shook my purse to make sure the card wasn't stuck in one of the pockets. I couldn't believe it! I searched the house and filing cabinet and still couldn't find either item. Later, after the transaction, I found the insurance card in plain sight on the end table next to the couch. I also found the registration behind the opened door in the laundry room. It was leaning up against the wall and was pulled out from behind the door just enough so that it could be seen. There's something fishy going on in this house!

May 28: I stood in the family room at about 12:20 A.M. and asked whatever was with me to give me a sign of its presence. It knocked about 30 seconds later. I recorded it.

> Note: I didn't realize until later on that by doing this I had probably unwittingly invited something more into my house…as if I didn't have enough intruders already!

June 5: I think this was the day something grabbed my breasts sometime in the night and squeezed them. It was dark and I couldn't see anything, but that is what it felt like. It was a very painful experience. This was something evil!

June 10: I tried to banish whatever is here, and it went away…no doubt. I felt more relaxed than I have for I don't know how long! It came back after a few hours.

June 15: On and off faint gnawing sound behind the nightstand in my bedroom. No sign of a mouse or like critter. Once again, I have had a pest control company coming to my home on a continual basis since I moved in. I've had mice in the garage at times, but my technician has ruled out any animals in my house both in the walls or otherwise.

June 26: This morning, before greeting the day, I heard knocking on the bedroom wall behind the loveseat. It seems like there is a lot of activity in that area. Now things are going on behind my headboard again…tapping sounds, like a long fingernail or claw performing the deed. It sometimes uses different rhythms with its tapping. Later in the day, I went out to the garage and the same board that had fallen backward before fell again. It fell in the same way and in the same place. Once again, it happened while my back was turned.

June 29: I attempted to smudge my house today armed with sage and a mantra I found online. I'd barely finished the job when there were three very loud, defiant knocks on the kitchen wall I was standing approximately six inches from. I called it a son of a bitch and told it I wasn't going to give up on my efforts to get rid of it.

About 12:30 A.M., it sounded as if the cross on the fireplace mantel in the family room on the other side of my bedroom wall was being moved…a dragging sound. I turned on my bed massager to hopefully drown out the noise. Then I heard what sounded like drum sticks being beaten together in the rhythm of the massager. It seemed as though sleep wasn't an option.

Around 4:00 A.M., I again felt what seemed to be an arm wrap around me. I told the wrongdoer to leave me alone, and he left. Then the tapping on the headboard started…

July 3: Quite a bit of pillow scratching at night.

July 10: The noise continues.

July 13: Again, I felt a presence in bed behind me...same song just another verse.

I'm becoming depressed. It's hard to be motivated to do anything.

July 14: I recited the Lord's Prayer over and over this evening...for about two hours. There was silence until the end of each recitation, and then there would be knocking on the walls. This happened every time I recited the Lord's Prayer. I finally gave up. I set up crosses throughout the house. Although there is a cross in the master bedroom, something stayed there with me last night.

I didn't even attempt to go to sleep. I tried leaving the light on in my bedroom, but the knocking continued. I finally turned off the light at about 4:00 A.M. I may have fallen asleep around 4:30 and was awoken at approximately 8:00 this morning to what sounded like someone clicking their tongue. Somehow, tongue clicking seems evil to me...very disturbing.

July 22: I was studying in my office around 5:00 P.M. when I went to the adjoining closet to get some printing paper. I returned to my chair and turned it around to face the printer. I heard some rustling going on behind me in the closet. It went on for approximately 30 seconds. It startled me, and although I took a sigh of relief when it stopped, I didn't turn around to see what was going on.

There was silence for about another 30 seconds and then I heard something heavy hit the carpeted floor directly behind me, making a loud thud. It occurred to me that something was trying to intimidate me. I sat there, realizing that whatever had dropped what was lying on the floor behind me was in close proximity to me, had once again shown its ability to manipulate things and was waiting for my response to its actions. I became unduly frightened considering what I have already been through but slowly turned around to find nothing more than a large new roll of silver duct tape standing in a rolling position on the carpet behind me. I had noticed it sitting on top of the filing cabinet in the closet when I grabbed my printing paper. It had been lying on its side.

The closet is a good six feet from where I was sitting. To the skeptic who may say it dropped off the filing cabinet and rolled to its destination directly behind me, that would be quite a journey! It would have had to land in the correct rolling position to exit the closet and continue its trip along a padded, carpeted floor. Then it would have needed to be elevated and dropped again right behind me...I only heard it drop once. The scariest part is that I thought I felt something looming over me. This is the first time I have fled my home. I called my daughter on the way and asked if I could spend the night, but when I got about a half mile from her house, I called her back and told her I was returning home. I couldn't let this thing get the best of me, and I wasn't sure it wouldn't follow me into her house.

> Note: I should mention that because of some of the things going on that seemed supernatural, I felt it necessary to do a bit of studying regarding demonic activity. I was doing so as the above-mentioned duct tape incident happened.

Upon my return, I was greeted by pounding on the walls and the sound like two drum sticks being hit together. I felt every hair on my body standing on end, and then it felt as if someone had placed their hands on the sides of my head and was applying pressure. I immediately started reciting the Lord's Prayer and continued doing so until I went to bed. During the recitation, something touched the back of my neck. The knocking didn't stop, but I became exhausted and went to bed around 12:20 A.M. and left the TV on. I slept without interruption until around 3:00 A.M., when I turned the TV off.

July 23: Around 5:00 A.M. I was awakened by knocking and once again started reciting the Lord's Prayer and went back to sleep for a couple hours.

At around 12:40 P.M., I started feeling like someone was dangling a string in a manner that tickled the back of my neck and upper back. I was fully clothed, but when this thing touches me in any way, it goes right through my clothing to my flesh, as if I'm unclothed. I heard a constant sound show consisting of knocking, thuds, taps, and other like sounds at a low intensity. I continued the day doing my usual household tasks trying to ignore the activity and occasionally reciting the Lord's Prayer.

I wrote up another prayer asking the Lord for forgiveness for my past lack of faith and other sins. I also asked that He rebuke whatever evil is in my home. Just as I was about to recite the written prayer, I heard the tongue clicking...it didn't deter me. I recited the prayer, on my knees, over and over before settling down for the night but continued to hear an impressive, lengthy repertoire of sounds and noises. I decided to try earplugs and took a sleeping pill.

July 27: I was able to get a paranormal research group to come to my home. Their main purpose was to find scientific and/or practical reasons for claims like mine. I probably wouldn't have had them come, but I had a four-hour recording that I had done one night a few weeks before where the noise hardly ever stops—knocking, whipping sounds, sounds like furniture moving...it's an amazing recording! They weren't interested in it. I guess it isn't proof to them inasmuch as they didn't do the recording.

I was honest with them about my past and that I'm bipolar. That probably only added credence to their already suspicious point of view. They were great people, though, and there were a couple of experiences they couldn't explain. One was the lighting above the stairs turning on apparently by itself as they headed down to the basement. The second was a knock one of the investigators and I heard as we walked by the dining room. **As far as they were concerned, there is nothing paranormal going on in my home.**

Their parting theory was that something may be "attached" to me. However, they took some pictures, did some recordings, and said they would get back in touch. They freely spent four hours of their time in my home and were a big help. They told me they were referring me to another group that they felt could be more of a help to me. Although they also take a scientific approach, they are more open-minded as to paranormal happenings.

> *Note: An "attachment," as it is referred to in paranormal terms, suggests that a living person has the energy of a negative dead person attached to them. More about this type of anomaly is included in Chapter 14.*

July 29: The paranormal investigators that were referred to me by the other group came by. He is a pastor and his wife a parapsychologist. They listened to my recording and seemed somewhat startled by it. They didn't seem to doubt that the activity was real and not something conjured up by me. The pastor walked through the house while his wife listened to the recording. Great people! No talk of money except from my mouth. I wanted to at least help by paying for the gas it took for them to get here and back home again. It was a long drive for them; they wouldn't hear of it.

> *Note: In brief, a parapsychologist attempts to investigate paranormal and psychic phenomena, which includes telepathy, precognition, clairvoyance, psychokinesis, near-death experiences, reincarnation, and apparitional experiences, etc., from a scientific, psychological point of view.*

August 5: I retired about 1:15 A.M. and turned on the bed massager hoping it would mask the potential noise that I suspected would permeate my night. Soon there was scratching and tapping on my headboard in sync with the rhythm of the massager. I turned off the massager and heard random knocks and taps. I firmly told the guilty party to stop, and it did. At 2:15 A.M., I was awakened by two very loud knocks coming from the master bathroom. I once again told the noisemaker to stop, and it did.

Somehow, I failed to mention an interesting experience I had recently. I had returned home from a quick trip to the grocery store, and

as I was walking past the wall that separates my master closet from the garage, I heard the faint sound of my vacuum cleaner running. I stopped dead in my tracks and slowly, deliberately tiptoed closer to the wall to get a better listen. As my ear was about to meet the wall, the noise abruptly stopped. This was extremely entertaining for me, and as I thought, upon further inspection, my master closet and vacuum cleaner I store there appeared to be just as I had left them.

August 6: I am coming to the realization that something here is listening to and understands my phone conversations. I know I sound like a lunatic, but I'm going to keep this in mind. Today I was talking to my daughter on the phone about a house cleansing that the last paranormal investigators to visit my home are setting up for me. Shortly after, I headed down to the basement and was greeted by two very loud crashes. It sounded as though something very large, like perhaps a dining room table, had fallen through the main floor into the basement. Of course, everything looked just fine! As I mentioned, it happened twice with a couple minutes between crashes. This was the loudest noise yet...it shook the house!

I found something disturbing on the sliding glass doors in the master bedroom today. It looks as though an animal with muddy claws has been scratching on the lower portion of the inside of the sliding glass door behind the loveseat. Dirty looking scratches over scratches over scratches. I know that something likes that part of the bedroom because I hear it there making quiet sounds like tapping, tinkering, and rustling noises at night. I often hear what sounds like scissors being manipulated. I think the dirty scratches have probably been there for a while and I haven't noticed. They look like they have been. I have no animals in my house...at least that I can see.

August 8: Not as noisy as usual today.

August 11: No noise except on my recorder while I was gone.

August 19: Still some noise during the day, but not so active at night.

August 23: I heard quiet noises behind the headboard while I was thinking of getting up this morning. **I also thought I saw a black animal-like figure about the size of a large dog zoom past me. I didn't see it straight on but out of the corner of my eye.**

August 26: It was quiet today except during the time I turned on the recorder and left for a while. The noise didn't stop. It sounded as though one of my freeloaders was venting...angry noise.

As I went out to the garage to get in the car, a metal rake that had been leaning against a wall in the garage fell straight backward in the same way as the aforementioned board has a couple of times. The rake is in a different area of the garage than the board. I didn't see it fall because my back was turned, but I heard it when it hit the floor.

August 29: I awoke about 7:30 A.M. to some tapping on the headboard. All I said was "Stop that," and the noise stopped immediately. It was quiet until I got up.

August 30: It's getting noisy.

September 4: I lose things constantly. I can be sitting on the couch switching TV channels with the remote control, set it down and not leave my seat, but somehow my remote seems to disappear. I look under the couch, pull up the cushions, and search there with no luck. I think to myself that I must have gotten up to do something and just forgotten, so I hunt all around the room with no results. I give up, shut the TV off manually, and turn around to see the remote sitting on the couch right where I thought I'd left it, in plain sight! This scenario has repeated itself many times.

Glasses are another story. I've lost up to three or four of them at a time, and they can be missing for weeks. Then I'll find all of them in one

easily seen, obvious place; not hidden...in plain sight. The strangest glasses situation came about recently when I lost a pair that I had been using all day. I hunted around for them but didn't want to take a lot of time searching, so I located another pair. I was in the garage, on my way out, when I noticed the glasses I'd been looking for under the windshield wiper of my car.

September 7: The pastor that is working with me came over this evening with a Catholic priest. We talked for a while about what has been going on here, and I shared some of my recordings with them since the priest had not yet heard them. They both agreed that there is something going on in my home. However, it was very quiet while they were here. In addition to blessing my house, the priest also blessed my crosses. It was such a pleasant evening, and I felt much more at peace after their visit.

September 8: Not a lot of noise today, but a lot of activity tonight.

September 13: This morning I felt a pulsating pain on one of my shoulders. The area affected was about the diameter of a quarter. I asked that whatever was causing the pain stop...the pain stopped immediately.

> *Note: There were periods of time when I became tired of journaling. There was always noise going on at varying degrees, day and night. I know this is repetitious but feel the need to mention that this was still the case.*

November 4: When I exited the shower this evening, I heard the hot water heater working harder than usual. I dismissed it, telling myself that I probably just don't generally take notice of its noise or that maybe I used too much hot water in the shower. I fixed some dinner, and when I turned on the water to begin the process of cleaning things up, it was scalding hot! I turned off the faucet and went downstairs to see what the water temperature was. It showed the thermostat placed at its coolest

setting! After the tap water cooled down, I made several trips up and down the stairs in an effort to find the right temperature. When it seemed right, I duct-taped the control.

I have also duct-taped the furnace on/off switch because the furnace kept turning off on its own. It seems as though the duct tape has taken care of the situation. I duct-taped the sprinkling system control box shut several weeks ago when I noticed the sprinkling system running at an unusual time of night and that the grass was exceedingly wet the next day. I wish I had noticed this sooner because a couple days after, I received a note on my front door telling me that I may have a leak somewhere, because my water usage was excessive... 23,000 more gallons than usual! Obviously, this had been going on for a while. My settings hadn't been changed and there was no logical reason for this. Fortunately, my sprinkling system is now turned off in preparation for winter.

Tonight, I smelled the faint scent of cigarettes and saw a thin veil of smoke between the kitchen and family room. In regard to cigarettes, although I am not a smoker, I sometimes feel a strong urge to smoke. I have recently started keeping a pack of Marlboro Lights hidden in the basement, and maybe once or twice a month, when I get the urge, I smoke one. On a side note, my paternal grandmother smoked cigarettes, and she did so secretively.

I've had a lot of light bulbs burn out lately. As I was changing some bulbs in the master bedroom, closet, and bathroom recently, I heard tapping that seemed to be coming from the chandelier over my bed. Because tapping is such a common sound, I noted it but went on with my work. Afterward, I went out to the garage, put the ladder away, and returned to find that one of the chandelier bulbs was out. I remembered the tapping sound I had heard just a few minutes earlier. It could be a coincidence, but maybe the tapping sound was the bulb being manipulated. I tightened the bulb, and it was fine. I went into the bathroom and noticed that, although I had just finished replacing all the burned-out bulbs in that location, another one was out. I tightened it, and it also came back to life.

My car has gone dead twice while sitting in the garage overnight since I bought it several months ago. Because it's new, I believe that I could be doing something to cause this. Maybe I've left an interior light on inadvertently…I don't know.

I often feel as though I'm walking through spider webs, especially in the basement. Although I realize that in any house, especially in a basement, there are going to be webs, this is like I've never experienced before. Keep in mind that I have a pest control company. If I find spiders in the house between service dates, I have them come out, and they take care of the problem. They do a great job, and I seldom see spiders or any kind of insect activity in my home. There have been times, in the basement, when I have felt like I'm walking through a tunnel of webs, but there is no physical evidence of webs on or around me.

Note: I have since learned that this kind of sensation can be a sign that I am in the presence of a ghost.

November 5: I was unable to keep an appointment with my psychotherapist today because my car battery was dead, so we handled the appointment over the phone. Because I'm almost certain that I have at least one boarder in my home that can hear and understand what I say and I wanted to speak to my therapist in private, I went outside on the patio. As I shut the sliding glass door from my master bedroom, I heard what sounded like two static electricity crackling sounds. I felt that my therapist and I had an eavesdropper.

After the session with my therapist, I walked over to the next-door neighbor's house to find out if there was anyone there who could help me recharge my car battery. Nobody was home, but as I was waiting for a possible response, I heard rhythmic tapping on the window next to their door…something was right there with me!

Later, after getting my car in running order, I turned on the digital recorder and left the house to run some errands. When I returned, I listened to it and heard a lot of activity around the house.

After an active, insightful day, it is evening, and it is unusually quiet.

November 7: Lately, there seems to be more activity in the basement. There's a lot of unexplainable noise coming from the duct work; there's also a lot of pounding and knocking. It sounds like someone is finishing that area of my house! I continue to hear the sound of furniture moving coming from the dining room area.

November 8: I was downstairs on the treadmill when I heard pounding on the heat duct directly over my head.

November 10: I'm working on the computer in my bedroom. I can hear pounding, the whipping sound (like a whip snapping), and the sound of furniture being dragged over the wood floor in the dining room. As usual, there is no sign of movement, and as soon as I peek outside my bedroom door to see what is going on, all noise stops and then starts again when I am no longer in a position to spy on the noisemaker.

November 11: While using the treadmill today, the power went off and on twice. I've been hearing what sounds like footsteps recently.

I was working on the computer in my bedroom this evening and heard what sounded like a squeaky door slowly opening and closing. Although I've heard it before, it's a less frequent phenomenon than some of the others. In actuality, none of my doors squeak.

November 12: The constant, unceasing knocking and tapping is driving me crazy. At night especially, I'm still hearing what sounds like a conversation between two humans coming from the basement. This isn't anything new, but it hasn't happened for a while. Although I can hear the voices of people conversing, as soon as I get close enough that I think I might be able to hear what's being said, the conversation abruptly stops.
Another light bulb burned out today.

November 13: I spoke to my sister on the phone this evening and complained about all the noise and how it is getting to be too much for me. It quieted down for a little while.

November 15: There has been knocking on the wall that separates the family room from my bedroom this evening. It's getting late, and I asked the culprit to stop. There was about a three-minute pause and then the noise started up again. It seems that one of my freeloaders has a very short attention span. Turning on the bed massager masks the knocking somewhat, but then the pillow scratching starts so that I can't sleep on my side, which is my typical sleeping position.

November 16: I'm experiencing a lot of face, ear, and upper eyelid itching. I'm getting very edgy and stressed. I went to bed early and went right to sleep but was soon awakened by two voices conversing with one another. As usual, it seemed to be coming from the basement. I headed down the stairs to get a closer listen, but the talking stopped before I got very close. I went back to bed, and it started right back up. I have also tried listening through the heat registers, but the talking stops before I can get my ear close enough to the register to listen.

November 17: This morning, I put my coffee in the microwave to reheat it and caused all kinds of racket. I quickly opened the door and found a spoon inside—not in the coffee cup, just randomly lying on the carousel inside. I can't say I'm sure I didn't inadvertently put it there, but such a thing has not happened before. A spoon is unnecessary because I drink my coffee black.

I'm still itching. I've stopped taking my new vitamins and quit using hair conditioner, but nothing's changed. I'm feeling the area pain that I've mentioned before, pain that can be located just about anywhere on my body but localized to about a quarter-size space. It is a pain that makes me wince and can go on from 30-60 seconds. I can ask whatever is causing the torture to stop, and the pain ceases. Sometimes, though, it just moves to another part of my body. This abuse is not accompanied by any marks.

It's about 10:30 A.M., and I will be going downstairs to exercise. There is so much noise down there right now, I dread it. I'm not afraid, just irritated by it.

November 18: Tonight, I prayed, read the scriptures, and read my mother's prayer book out loud before I went to bed. I hope it helps.

November 19: Lots of knocking.

November 21: My two sons spent the night in my family room. They were here to conduct their own little investigation and possibly influence whatever is here to leave. Nothing of significance happened, but I was able to sleep.

November 23: I was awakened at 2:30 A.M. by tapping. It wasn't very loud but was annoying. I used earplugs. I don't like them, but they're sometimes better than the alternative.

November 24: About 9:15 A.M., there was tapping in my office while I was doing paper work. At 10:15 A.M. the lights in the office went off and then on. A little later, the TV channel got changed. I'm certain I had nothing to do with any of it!

November 25: It has been a very noisy evening and night.

November 28: I spent the night at my daughter's house. It was nice to get a good night's sleep.

November 29: The pest woke me up this morning earlier than I would have liked, but I slept better than usual.

December 2: The noise around here has been a bit subdued. I've been able to get a decent night's sleep for two nights in a row!

December 3: One of the bathroom light bulbs burned out Thursday. The one right next to it burned out Saturday; they both burned out as I passed by them. **A light bulb above the stairs fizzled out tonight. It seems like I just changed it! On a side note…it is my mother's birthday.**

December 4: I got involved in doing some work in the guest room today and didn't leave that area until after dark. There were no lights on in the rest of the house, and it seemed as if my roomie may have been confused about the time. The nonstop knocking generally doesn't start until I go to bed, but it began about 7:00 P.M. I walked into the family room and couldn't help laughing.

"You're a little early tonight, I think you're a bit confused" I said.

Since I tend to believe the knocking is an attempt to keep me awake, I thought maybe because the house was dark and quiet, the rapper thought I was in bed for the night. It was also a very stormy night. Maybe this anomaly had been energized by the thunder, lightning, and pouring rain earlier in the evening. At any rate, the knocking stopped and then started in again about 12:00 A.M. when I went to bed.

December 5: So much noise in my bedroom tonight! Lots of tapping on the headboard and pillow scratching. I turned on the bed massager, and within a few minutes, I heard rhythmic knocking. I wonder if this is the same anomaly that adds knocks between my steps on the treadmill.

December 7: I heard whistling while I was downstairs today. Not a tune, just a series of short whistles. Both of my parents were whistlers.

December 8: I slept well. The only sound I heard was a little quiet tapping.

December 9: Another quiet night!

December 10: I'm hearing what sounds like tapping on the headboard tonight, but it sounds like it is right next to my ear.

Another light bulb went out in the bathroom today, but it just needed to be screwed in tighter. Another one burned out.

December 13: Later this morning, I heard a very loud crash at the bottom of the stairs. It sounded like a large piece of furniture had fallen from a distance and landed there; it shook the house. After the initial shock, I went downstairs, and as I expected, everything was just as it was the last time I was down there.

Not a pleasant night. The night owl spent a lot of time in my room around the computer. I also felt a tickling sensation…like a thread was being dangled back and forth lightly touching my face.

December 15: I talked to my friend, the parapsychologist, this evening. I was baking cookies, and while I was on the phone with her, the oven lightbulb burned out. She's been a good friend.

December 18: I saw my therapist today. I've become quite a bore. All I want to talk about are my paranormal encounters. He and the parapsychologist have both told me I need to ignore what's going on.

    After seeing my therapist, I ran some errands and came home. As I opened the entry door from the garage and entered the laundry room, I heard three loud thumps, like someone taking a 2x4 and lifting it with great force to hit what would be the basement ceiling right under my feet. I could feel the floor shake! This thing knows what I do, and it knows what people tell me. It becomes angry at very appropriate times. It doesn't want to be ignored.

    Later, I dropped one of my night time pills…it's gone. I went so far as to clean the bathroom in an effort to find it. I took everything off the counter, wiped it down, and swept the floor. It could have found its way down the sink drain, I guess, but I doubt it. Maybe the invisible psycho needed it more than I did!

I was awakened in the night by a swift slap on the butt. Although that part of my body was not exposed, as I've mentioned before, somehow, when I get touched, I feel it as though there is no clothing involved. A few minutes later, it happened again. I also heard the voices coming from the basement. I've set up my digital recorder down there on several occasions, but the conversationalists don't converse when I'm recording.

December 22: I was in the basement exercising. The light bulb above the treadmill was flickering, and then I heard what sounded like a siren. It sounded like it was right there in the basement. It was a quiet day after that.

December 26: I left my recorder on in the basement while I was gone. I have an hour of noise that didn't cease. It was repetitive and continuous. I also heard what sounded like two small objects hit the floor and later noticed that a small spool of thread and an old glob of putty could have been the droppings.

December 29: Since experiencing paranormal activity in my house, I've been noticing some odd marks showing up on my arms, hands, legs and feet. I've never experienced anything like them before. They appear to be fang marks, and they could be duplicated by someone taking a standard-size staple and jabbing it into their skin until it bleeds. I have seen other similar marks, but if it itches or is swollen, I see such blemishes as a couple of bug bites or something other than what I call "fang marks."

Several times this month, I have seen creatures scurrying by out of the corner of my eye. Although they differ in shape, they are always black. I try not to take things I see out of the corner of my eye too seriously, but they sure seem real.

December 30: I'll be doing just fine, and then, when I least expect it, I'll remember something in my past, including my childhood, that makes me feel guilty and I can hardly stand it. This can happen day or night and happens frequently. It's nothing new, but I seem to have been plagued by it more than usual today and tonight.

I have a family photo gallery of sorts in the formal dining room. Several months ago, I decided to choose some of my childhood photos to fill three small, pewter, oval frames held together by small chains on either side. I found four small pictures of my parents, paternal grandparents, and me. They were individual pictures of each of them, posing on a large rock, holding me on their lap; I was nine months old. Because there were only three frames, I decided to leave the picture of my father and me out. I hung it in a nice spot where it filled a gap between two larger framed photos. It was a nice addition! However, I have noticed a seepage of some sort forming on the wall beneath the last frame attached to the chains. It is approximately two inches long and about an eighth of an inch wide.

I've tried wiping it off with a damp cloth to no avail. I've also tried using a spot remover that removes candle wax and gum among other things, and that didn't work either. It is a very tacky, gooey substance that seems to be there to stay. I'm not taking the frames down because the substance is translucent and not very noticeable. I'm going to keep my eye on it though...it's strange.

CHAPTER TEN

2013

January 3: This past week I've needed to replace the batteries in two of my remote controls. One of them ended up missing for two days. I looked in, on, and around the couch many times...even lifted the cushions. I finally found it under some papers on the couch where I'd been looking for it all along. Now my bed remote is missing. I'm headed downstairs to exercise... sure hope the treadmill is still there! **The problems with the furnace have started up again. Apparently, the duct tape isn't working after all...not a surprise.**

January 4: As I was heading downstairs around 2:30 P.M., one of my housemates was beside me knocking on the wall. I heard loud knocking seemingly on the ceiling just above my head while I was on the treadmill. I would hear a knock, then nothing for about eight seconds, and then another knock. This went on for about 10 minutes, at which time the knocking became progressively fainter until it stopped.

January 6: Great day! I didn't lose anything and felt less confused than usual.

January 7: Noisy night. Not loud noisy, but agitating noisy; faint, but constant knocking. I told the rapper to STOP, which it did for about a minute! Then, a little later on, I started hearing the conversationalists. I checked outside to see if the voices could be coming from a neighbor's TV or radio. They weren't coming from outside, but inside, as has always been the case.

January 9: I was awakened by loud, exuberant, rhythmic knocking. It was as if someone was saying, "Get up, let's go! It's going to be a great day." Honestly, I wasn't feeling it. The persistent knocking ceased as it usually does once I get out of bed. A little later this morning, I heard a loud, house trembling crash in the basement. This is happening more and more. I called my sister, and there was a lot of noise going on during our conversation. A little later, I heard a very loud knock come from the dining room.

I went downstairs to go through stuff and get a donation ready for the Vets. This was one of my strangest experiences yet. Whatever entity decided to join me down there was very active...off the wall, and seemed to be enjoying my company. It really wasn't cool on my part, but I must admit that I enjoyed the interaction as well. I was playing some of my favorite music. It's a bit dark, sometimes sad and touching, sometimes loud and angry. It is music that makes me "feel." I got the distinct impression that whatever was with me was "feeling" it too!

We were down there from about 7:00 to 9:00 P.M., at which time I went upstairs and set about doing some cleaning, taking down Christmas tree ornaments, and other little tidbits of work. My sister called, and we had a nice conversation...the call ended about 10:00. I continued working until about 11:30. It seemed as though my sidekick was no longer with me but stayed downstairs. It was time for bed, and I did my nightly ritual of reading the scriptures, praying, and reciting excerpts from my mother's Episcopal prayer book. I then decided to listen to some of my recordings when I started hearing thumps, cracking sounds, and knocking all around me. This went on for about an hour. I decided to try to get some sleep in spite of all the ruckus. I dozed off and was awakened with a start by the sound of pots and pans banging as if falling on each other...very loud!

Above me was a sight that I've seen before: colored, debris-like objects coming at me from the ceiling—not dropping slowly but violent,

62

"coming at me" flashes. Then it seemed as though the room was spinning, as if I were lying on my bed after drinking too much. Then I saw something shaped like a tornado above me, only upside down. I saw large and small pebble-like shapes swirling around me; they were brownish gold in color with rounded edges. All of this seemed to be cartoonish. I think the entire scenario lasted about three minutes. Honestly, I don't know what this was. I got up, took a sleeping pill, and wrote this before falling asleep. Very strange day!

January 11: The furnace guy is coming out today to fix my furnace. I went downstairs to monitor exactly what it is doing so as to better explain the problem to him. I took some paperwork down with me and sat at a table I have down there. It was silent. The back of my chair was approximately 18 inches from the basement wall. Then, out of nowhere, right behind me, I heard what sounded like something very heavy—like a piece of furniture with large heavy legs—being dragged directly behind me along the particleboard floor. It was loud enough that it made my ears ring, and I could feel the vibration as it was being moved. My reaction was kind of interesting. I raised my eyes up from my paperwork until the noise stopped and then simply continued with what I was doing.

The noise didn't scare me, but it did startle me. In reality, I've heard that noise a lot, but never up close and personal. The furniture mover had never invaded my space like that before! It was an unbelievable experience, but one that can't be denied.

January 12: The furnace repair has been successful…that's a good thing.

Today, something has been following me around, scratching on walls, knocking, and making static electricity sounds. It has been obnoxious, but nothing I can't handle; tonight is different. I'm so tired!

January 13: Last night wasn't bad to begin with. I could hear noise traveling from my bedroom, to the family room, to the bathroom. It was keeping me awake. **Around 2:00 A.M., I felt something over the top of me. Then it** seemed as if I was being used as a punching bag...very quick punches to my gut. The weird part is that it felt like the punches went right through me...as if I was the one without any body mass, and it was the human! It went on for about 30 seconds, and then it stopped. I rolled over on my side and went to sleep. It isn't that I wasn't disturbed by the whole thing...just too tired to care. There was no pain involved and no bruises or marks of any kind when I awakened this morning. This was a first. I've never in my life felt anything like that!

January 15: Some of my journal notes have been missing for a couple days. They turned up today, right out in the open! Some freak of nature has been spending a lot of time in my bedroom. I was attacked again last night just as I have been many times before. I tried to call it a son of a bitch but was being squeezed so tight that I didn't have the breath to speak. However, I was finally able to utter the words, "Dear Lord, help me!" and the abuse stopped.

I was able to get a couple hours of sleep this morning between 9:00 and 11:00 A.M. It has been so noisy around here, and I'm exhausted. I don't know what I'm dealing with when I'm attacked. It just doesn't seem like my attacker is the same anomaly that is here most of the time.

Today, I noticed that the closet in the guest bedroom was not as it usually is. The toy basket was out of place. Also, a chair that sits against the dining room wall was moved out. I haven't seen large things out of place before; i.e., when I know that I haven't moved them. Then something amazing happened.

I was in the office getting some jellybeans out of a gumball machine I keep stocked up for the grandkids, and a black one fell to the floor. I found it, and as I reached to pick it up, it was literally grabbed, as if a human hand had grabbed it, but the hand was unseen. It wasn't my imagination...this was truly amazing! I looked around for it, knowing full well I wouldn't find it. This little incident gave me some insight as to what happens to my earrings when I drop them. I think I caught the poltergeist red-handed, so to speak...not a common thing to experience.

January 18: Things settled down for a while last night, but when I woke up early this morning I moved my arm ever so slightly, and that prompted some immediate noise. That's how it started out…like a puppy that wants to go for a walk in the morning before their owner is awake. When the critter sees any sign of life, it gets excited and won't give in until it gets its way.

Once again, it becomes more and more clear to me as time goes by that at least one of my intruders can hear me speak, even in a whisper, anywhere in the house. This entity seems to be aware of everything I do and say, often responding to things I mention when talking on the phone or to myself. I become more and more sure of this as time goes by. Its keen senses and intelligence never cease to amaze me.

Well, tonight, half a sleeping pill, a prayer, and I'll read another chapter in the Book of Matthew. After that, I'll watch TV for a little while. I hate to face the silence, because as soon as I do, it is taken up by whatever.

January 22: I've had a little relief for a couple days. There has been more noise during the day and not so much at night. It's good to have a little peace.

As I was heading for the stairs after using the treadmill today, I heard something fall behind me. It was a small yellow dish that my eldest son made for me when he was in grade school. The dish has been sitting flat on a shelving unit in the basement since I moved into the house. It was not near the edge of the shelf, but more toward the middle where I put it when I moved in. I put it back where it had been before it dropped.

A few days ago, I lost an earring. As with the jellybean, and many earrings before it, I dropped it on the floor, and it disappeared. I didn't witness it disappear as with the jellybean, but I couldn't find it. I asked that it be returned but really didn't expect such an occurrence. This morning I was awakened by sparking sounds in the closet and went to see what was going on. I felt that my earring had been returned, and I found it neatly placed in the jewelry box…that is amazing!

It has been VERY noisy in the dining room tonight. It sounded like the buffet was being messed with and went on for about a half hour. I'm now hearing quiet knocks behind my headboard.

January 23: I went into my bedroom and set up the computer, and the radio in the laundry room started playing. It didn't scare me. It made me laugh. I was reading the scriptures, and I heard a crackling sound that came from the direction of the chandelier. It startled me a little.

January 24: NO NOISE!

January 29: I'm hearing noises, but not loud ones. I heard one of the free-loaders in my bedroom last night, and when I decided to settle down, I mentioned that I sure hoped it wasn't going to keep me awake all night, and it left. I heard the voices in the basement...loud but not unbearable. I feel like at least one of the aberrations I'm dealing with has the ability to manipulate things like TV's, boomboxes, computers, cell phones, etc. That's why it's so difficult to determine exactly what the voices are. I do keep my boombox down there!

January 31: I heard three loud crashes this morning.

February 1: Fairly quiet today. Just enough noise to let me know I'm not alone.

February 2: I heard quite a commotion this morning around the "witching hour" (3:00 A.M.). I didn't get much sleep after that. It was a quiet day.

> *Note: Witching Hour: An occult belief that refers to the time at which entities such as witches, demons, and ghosts are thought to appear and be at their most powerful. While it seems most believe that this period lasts from 3:00 a.m. to 4:00 a.m., this theory is not set in stone.*

February 3: My missing deodorant has reappeared. I always have two sticks of deodorant so that I have one when the other one turns up missing! This kind of stuff, in my opinion, is poltergeist activity, and it doesn't bother me. **I went downstairs, and the little decorative yellow plate that landed on the floor**

the other day was back on the floor again. I've been wondering if a benevolent spirit, such as my mother, is trying to let me know that my son who made the plate needs my help. I sent him a text inquiring as to his well-being and included an inspirational thought. I've had some concerns about him for a while and have meant to do this before now.

February 4: I haven't been hearing a lot of knocking at night lately. I've asked that I be left alone at night and that I wouldn't mind being awakened around 9:00 in the morning. This morning I slept until about 9:30 A.M., at which time I was awakened by about 30 seconds of loud knocks. It made me chuckle.

This afternoon I heard gnawing, scratching sounds in/on the office walls. When I hear that, I feel evil around me. I don't believe it is what I refer to as a poltergeist.

February 5: Another fairly quiet day. I was gone for a time.

February 6: It is 1:05 A.M. As I'm writing, there is something behind me...it feels menacing.

February 7: While on the treadmill, I heard three very loud crashes. I'm not sure it wasn't caused by the washing machine, hot water heater, or something not paranormal. It's the nature of "three" sounds like that together that cause me concern. I'm still hearing scratching and gnawing sounds in/on the wall that separates the dining room and office. I've had this phenomenon checked out more than once by my pest control company. They always tell me there is nothing in the wall.

> *Note: Many demonologists, exorcists, and others involved with the*
> *supernatural believe that three knocks, or other such sounds, are*
> *often made by demons as a mockery of the Holy Trinity.*

February 10: I've had a couple quiet days, but it has been noisy tonight. Once again, there seems to be a conversation going on downstairs.

Part of what I think is going on here is that my house is on a piece of property that has had some bad history. However, I think that someone else could have bought this property and never had the kind of experiences I am having. Because of my past with mental illness and the paranormal world, I am susceptible to things that others are not.

February 11: It was a fairly quiet day, but the activity began in my bedroom as I started preparing to go to bed. I felt as though my ear was being pinched, and I could hear knocking in the dining room. I told it to stop, and it did. After a few minutes, the knocking started again, and again, I told it to stop; then something came into my bedroom and attacked me while I was in bed. As usual, I was rendered paralyzed and unable to speak. It was as if it had enveloped me and was smothering me. When it stopped, I turned over, hoping it was done with me for the night. Within a few minutes, the knocking started up again, and again I told it to stop, and it did, but I was then attacked in the same way again. I told my assailant to stop the attacks and the knocking and to get out of my house and that if it didn't leave, I was going to find a way to get rid of it!

I dozed off. I can't remember the dream in its entirety, but in essence it seemed that this same unseen demon was continuing to wreak havoc. I can't remember all the things it did, but I remember that it brought ants into my house. Then it took the form of my mother, but I knew what it was doing. My dream continued as I found myself in a restaurant with "my mother" and some of my grandchildren. One of my grandchildren mentioned that it was my mother's birthday and I said something unkind because I knew that what was before me was not her. At some point in the dream, a dog showed up. Upon awakening at 5:30 A.M., I got up knowing full well that things would only get worse if I didn't. I started hearing banging on the heat ducts. This is something that I haven't mentioned much except in my journaling, because no one believes me about the ducts. There are all kinds of noises that heat ducts make, but rhythmic banging isn't one of them! The banging stopped around 6:30 A.M.

February 13: I left for an appointment with my shrink, and when I got back around 4:00 P.M., it looked as though things like pens, a Kleenex box, and a can of furniture polish had been thrown around my bedroom. As I recall, all these items were there when I left, but not on the floor. However, I can't be sure I didn't just get in a hurry and do it myself.

February 14: I woke up this morning, and things had been shifted around in my room.

February 15: Fairly quiet today but getting noisy tonight.

February 17: A few things I've noticed recently. Plugs unplugged, duct tape stuck on the basement floor, a night light unplugged and plugged back in upside down.

February 19: Sometimes, I hear taps on the wall in the master bathroom stool room. I've tried to explain it away, but I can't. The tapping is consistent but stops when I knock back at it. It will sheepishly start up again and keep it up until I knock or leave. One thing I am painfully aware of in my present state is that I have no privacy.

The poltergeist can be reasoned with. I think it has the capability of causing flooding and electrical problems, but it is not evil. At its best, it is entertaining; at its worst, it costs me a lot of money in household repairs. What is evil here is nothing more than that. There are no redeeming qualities in a demon. They are nothing but bad. I believe that if I could get a good look at my attacker, it would be a dark figure. I've seen darkness above me when I wake up at night sometimes. It looks like a dark cloud hovering over me.

February 20: The random things I find on the basement floor continue to add up. The little yellow plate has again found its way there.

March 1: For the past week, things have quieted down. I had rotator cuff surgery on my right arm February 26 and have been recuperating. It feels like something is here with me, but its noise is subdued. In spite of added medication in the form of pain pills, things are not going missing.

March 7: I have a couple of friends here from out of state. They are visiting for a few days. The gal mentioned to me that while using the guest bathroom this afternoon, she heard what sounded like a marble rolling around in the bathroom ceiling. In reality, there is insulation above the ceiling, and a marble rolling around up there isn't feasible. However, I have heard the same thing in that bathroom...so nice to have it confirmed!

Speaking of marbles, although I can't recall the exact dates, I have been awakened by the sound of marbles falling inside the wall behind my headboard in the master bedroom. I remember one time in particular. I could hear them dropping and bouncing like marbles do when they hit the floor from a distance. It sounded like an amazing number of them, more and more falling, ceiling to floor. I played possum, so to speak, for a good 15 seconds, but when I moved ever so slightly, the noise stopped as abruptly as anything I've ever heard. Although such an incident couldn't actually occur, that is what it sounded like...amazingly so!

Note: I believe both marble incidents were brought on by the poltergeist.

March 8: Around 2:00 A.M., I was awakened by the sound of harpsichord music. I know how familiar this sounds. Harpsichord music is often played in old horror flicks, but, nonetheless, that is what I heard. It was so loud, and I ran around the house trying to find where it was coming from. It would travel from room to room as if to confuse me. It originally sounded like it was coming from the basement, but when I followed it there, it faded and sounded like it was upstairs. This is a common phenomenon that goes on with a lot of the noise in my house.

The music lasted for about ten minutes. As I was running around opening and closing doors, including the front door to make sure the

point of origin wasn't outside, I remembered that I had house guests and became concerned that I might have awakened them.

In the morning, when I joined my friends in the kitchen for coffee, I apologized for the noise I felt I may have caused while running around in the night. I began to explain that I had heard some rather odd music and was trying to find its point of origin. As soon as I said the word "music" my friend responded with a certain amount of excitement that she had heard it too. She said she thought it was coming from outside and had opened the guest room window only to realize that was not the case. She described it as "old funeral music." I love it when someone besides myself experiences my haunting. NOT that I like to have anyone become uneasy here. It's just that being able to have something like this confirmed by someone else is such a boon!

March 15: I haven't written much lately because there hasn't been much going on. The only thing that has been bothering me is a pain that sometimes feels like a pinch and other times the quarter-size pain I've mentioned before.

Today I left for a short time and set up my camcorder to see if I could pick up any activity. I left the door to the basement open and didn't set the alarm because I had the windows open, which disables the security system. It was quiet except for one big bang at the beginning and one at the end of the recording.

March 19: I went downstairs to exercise for the first time since my surgery. I turned on the boombox anticipating the DVD I listened to the last time I was down there. Instead, a preacher program was on...no static, perfect channel placement. I don't listen to the radio...just my DVD's. Maybe this radio station IS what I sometimes hear at night when I hear talking. It was, indeed, a religious talk show! I'm really getting a kick out of this. Maybe the voices have been the boombox being skillfully manipulated by something all along!

March 20: I've been noticing bloody spots and scratches on my face and body. Too many to disregard.

March 25: I returned home from the hospital yesterday after being gone from Friday until Sunday due to stomach pains. I went downstairs and heard three knocks, then another three upstairs.

I was using the printer to make some copies. I left the office and returned after a few minutes to find the first two copies on the floor. The printing was a mess!

I'm hearing subdued knocking tonight…no rhythm, one knock at a time. I also just heard what sounded like glass breaking directly above my head as I sit here typing.

April 4: It's been a decent day. There's been enough activity to make me aware of at least one of my pesky roommates, but not too crazy. I've started leaving the TV off more often and asked what I believe is the poltergeist, once again, to make its noise during the day instead of at night. **I continue to believe that the poltergeist is not the one that is ill-intentioned. I believe the attacks, all physical harm, and loud unceasing knocking is either a demon, an angry ghost, or both.**

April 6: I was awake most of the night. It's funny how at least one of my night owls works. My night will start out with quiet knocks. If I remain still, the unseen seems to get bored and goes elsewhere in the house—generally, the kitchen and family room areas where I can hear it messing around.

A while later, it will return to my bedroom and knock again. The knocks will be closer together and louder. Sometimes it will give up, and sometimes it will continue until I acknowledge its presence in some way. This night owl doesn't seem to be able to discern whether I'm asleep or just ignoring it. I experienced this first-hand last night, and I have recordings that also confirm it.

April 8: I've been having some work done in the basement. The carpenter came and finished putting up some new insulation today, and there was knocking all night! My guess is that at least one of my housemates isn't happy with the insulation.

April 9: Constant knocking all night.

April 10: Today I spoke very sternly to whatever was in earshot about the constant knocking at night. I stated that I don't know who/what is causing it but that the knocking at night has to stop. I stated that this is my house and that includes the basement and that I have the right to do whatever I want with it. I suggested that if one of them wanted to communicate, they knock once. There was no reply.

I ignored the freeloaders for the rest of the day. I bought a cheap fan in hopes that the white noise would help at night. That and the bathroom fan may do the trick. I hate the earplugs. At least one of my roomies seems to know when I'm using them because I've been experiencing something nudging me while I'm in bed, I assume to awaken me or get my attention when the earplugs block the noise.

Aside from keeping me awake at night and making noise during the day, what I've been dealing with lately hasn't done anything to hurt me. **My hair is being played with a little more than usual...doesn't faze me.**

April 13: It's 11:15 P.M., and as is often the case, something is in the bedroom with me. I hear it and feel it...I see nothing, and I can't get warm. I need to bring up a few things that continue:

I still see creepy animal-like black things out of the corner of my eye. I recently saw one that appeared to be a wild boar; it was the only one I got a good look at. They zip by me so fast! I also continue to see a dark shadow above my bed on the ceiling sometimes. It doesn't have any particular form, and I think it could be the shadow of something that isn't paranormal but can't come up with an answer as to what that might be. I also see large flies that silently, slowly fly by at a low level and then disappear. Their bodies are about the size of a black bean. Although I've seen them often throughout my time in this house, I've never found one dead as I have the more common house flies.

April 14: I took half a sleeping pill last night. I woke up at 4:05 A.M. but had no problem going back to sleep. I recently purchased an alarm clock that plays nature and white noise sounds. I had hoped it would help me sleep, but needless to say, it couldn't begin to compete with the noise around here! Anyway, I keep it on a dresser near my bed set on low brightness to enable me to see the time. I was awakened by the nature sounds setting at 7:30 A.M. I had not set the alarm. I reached for the clock to turn it off, but the sound stopped before I could lay a hand on it. A few minutes later, I started hearing knocks coming from the crawl space.

I've also been awakened from time to time by what sounds like an amazing number of small pebbles falling inside the wall, ceiling to floor, behind my headboard. The last time this happened, I opened my eyes but remained still for about three seconds in sheer amazement. Then, realizing I was awake, whatever had caused the noise stopped it as clearly and cleanly as to render the entire room silent. I continue to believe incidents such as this and the marble incidents are brought on by the poltergeist.

April 16: I'm trying to ignore the noise around me. I'm hearing quiet knocks and sundry unexpected sounds. **Two of the most dramatic deliveries for the day, was the sound of something fairly heavy, like a large chair or end table falling from a distance on to the family room floor at about 8:00 P.M. Then, about 10:30 P.M., it sounded like a pile of papers had landed on the entry floor just outside my office where I had been most of the evening.** No sign of either activity…just a little sound show. I went to bed about 12:50 A.M. and started reading the scriptures aloud. There were a couple taps as I started to read. No noise as I read.

Throughout the night, I heard what sounded like furniture moving and the usual voices coming from the basement. Maybe the conversationalists are telling the furniture mover where to place things!

April 17: Lots of noise today, but I'm trying to ignore it. **I saw what appeared to be a couple orbs, which I haven't seen before except in my videos. I** saw them in my peripheral vision.

Note: An orb is a spherical ball of light most often seen in videos and photographs. Although there is generally a logical explanation for them, i.e., dust, snow, rain, insects, reflection, lens flare, etc., they are a subject of interest by those who study the paranormal. Because they are often seen in conjunction with paranormal activity, they are believed by many a ghost hunter to be associated with ghosts and other anomalies.

I felt my hair being messed with tonight when I said my prayers. I also felt the quarter-size pain I often experience between the thumb and forefinger of my left hand. This was unusual, both in the sense that I was interrupted during my prayer and in that I have not felt that pain on my hand before.

I'm also experiencing cold drafts. My house is drafty, but I'm talking about something that seems to come from nowhere. This is becoming a common occurrence.

I'm hearing noise coming from the basement. It's not as bad as when the noise is in my room, but it still keeps me awake.

April 19: I've been hearing a lot of subtle sounds throughout the day that let me know I'm not alone. I also noticed some deep cuts in the kitchen floor today that I haven't seen before. They could be caused by something sharp like knives or scissors being dropped to the floor, points down. I'm not certain I haven't caused them and just not taken notice. I certainly drop things occasionally. A couple light bulbs in the master closet have gone out.

I've been hearing a lot of radio-type noise, faint music, and the conversationalists throughout the day, which is unusual; I generally hear these sounds at night. I'm fairly certain at this point that the conversationalists are in fact the boombox being manipulated by something. I leave things as they are down there because quenching my curiosity is more important to me than the disruption the voices cause me. I am equally awestruck by the ability this enigma has to detect every attempt I make to catch it in the act and stop the conversation before I can witness or clearly hear what is causing it. It isn't infallible, though…forgetting to change the boombox back to where my settings were after I had been gone for a time has led to my current thinking and possible answer as to what is probably going on.

I had a handyman over today to install fluorescent lighting in the basement. After he left, there was more banging and knocking than usual in that area of the house. This could very well be an expression of angst over yet another change by the freeloader that hangs out down there!

I went to bed early to watch TV. I heard something scurrying from corner to corner in my bedroom. It sounded like a caged animal trying to find its way out. I felt the area pain a couple times but was able to end my agony by ordering the responsible party to stop. I slept fairly well.

April 20: I heard some rhythmic, quiet knocking this morning. Later, I went downstairs for my daily dose of the treadmill, and it was quiet for the entire 45 minutes I was there! In fact, it was quiet for the rest of the evening.

April 21: It was quiet last night and most of today. I decided to do some cleaning in the basement and noticed that a bit of sudsy water had come up through the drain near the hot water heater. Since I was doing laundry, I thought it must be coming from the washer draining. I know that poltergeists are known for causing flooding problems, and this worries me a little. I heard one quiet knock as I was cleaning it up. I did another load of laundry and checked downstairs as the washer was draining. Again I noticed sudsy water coming up from the drain. I'll try using less detergent.

My car keys went missing yesterday. Since I didn't have the time to look for them, I used the spares, which I keep in a wooden box with a lot of other keys. I very deliberately and consciously put them back where they belonged when I returned home and began a search for the original set. I checked my purse and coat pockets and looked under furniture and every other place I could think of but couldn't find them. I gave up but later needed to take a drive, and when I went to get the spares, the original set was in the key box along with them. The interesting thing is that while I was looking for my keys,

I thought to myself that I should ask the thief to put them where I could find them. I had looked through that box three times before, dumped out its contents, and didn't see the original set of keys. As crazy as it sounds, I often wonder if at least one of my boarders can read my mind.

I recently lost my journal notes again and haven't found them yet. There were times when these kinds of tricks got out of hand and I would ask the trickster to stop and, to my surprise, things would settle down for a while. Although I believe this could still be an alternative, I sometimes prefer to let things be in the interest of learning more about what haunts me.

I've heard a few noises but have been gone for the better part of the day.

April 22: Very quiet, almost like I'm alone.

April 23: Last night, as I was getting ready for bed, I heard what sounded like the clinking of pieces of glass. It was like what one would hear from a glass windchime in a slow breeze and seemed to be coming from the decorative lighting I call a chandelier. It would seem that this light fixture yields many pleasant sounds. In reality, what appears to be a chandelier is merely a plastic façade of such. If it were real, the clinking glass sound could be made by two or more of the crystals being manipulated to touch each other by a breeze or an invisible hand, but there is no movement involved. I think it is just one of many sounds that what I call a poltergeist makes at will. If the sound was being made by the lighting above my bed, it would be the sound of plastic hitting plastic. The trickster that it is sometimes makes sounds that objects near me could make. If this is the case with the façade above my bed, the joke is on the noisemaker!

Radio/TV sounds, music, and what sounded like newscasts invaded my sleep during the night. At about 4:30 A.M., I heard two knocks, then a pause, then five knocks.

I've mentioned that I've been nudged awake sometimes. This morning, I woke up to my arm being lifted up from my side at the elbow in a repetitive, uncontrollable way; that is, controlled by something other than myself.

April 24: Since having the fluorescent lighting installed in the basement, I've noticed that they have been on when first entering the basement the next day. This has happened three days in a row. The thing is, I check all the lights before I go to bed. I am fastidious about this. I'll say it could be me leaving them on, but I don't really believe it. Sometimes I check the doors and lights two or three times AFTER I go to bed as well.

April 25: The day was quiet. The handyman was here doing a few things for me, and I asked him to change two light bulbs that had gone out in my closet. There are two light globes in the closet, each containing two light bulbs. Both bulbs under one of the globes were burned out. Anyhow, after he changed them, I switched the lights on and one of the light bulbs under the other light globe flickered out and needed to be replaced.

There was knocking all night. I also changed nightgowns twice to accommodate the difference in temperature that was taking place in my bedroom… fooling with the thermostat didn't help at all. At one point, I felt what seemed like a felt tip pen being guided from my left hip to my navel. It felt as though my skin was exposed, but I was fully covered. No pain, no marks…just a strange sensation.

April 27: This morning, I awakened to an electrical problem in the master bathroom. The stool room and ceiling lights all work; all seven lights above the mirror are not working.

I can't help believing that the sudsy drain in the basement and the seven lights that aren't working in the master bathroom are due to poltergeist activity. Some believe these energies are master plumbers and electricians! I left for a couple hours and stewed over my situation the entire time I was gone. I got home, walked into the house, went into the basement, started shouting obscenities at whatever was in earshot, and told the troublemaker to leave. As I turned the corner to go back upstairs, I heard a terrible crash. A fairly large over-door wall decoration I had hung on the basement wall above the stairway appeared to have been thrown to the ground and was broken into three pieces. There is no way its being thrown to the floor could have caused the earth-shattering level of noise I heard. Once again, a façade, merely a form of polystyrene, overlaid with a thin wood veneer. It's a strong material, and it took a lot of force to break into three pieces, but I laughed and told my roommate its antics didn't scare me!

I called the parapsychologist who helps me out in times like this, and she helped me to realize that I could be blaming my problems on an innocent party and that perhaps an apology might be in order. She also told me she felt I should not be uncomfortable talking to whatever it is directly. Also, that I should use the pronouns us and we when talking to it. I did as she suggested. I believe I have an angry ghost and a poltergeist...I don't know how to tell them apart.

April 29: Another quiet night...so nice! However, I had an amazing experience today. I was on the treadmill, and I witnessed a small, solid pinecone wreath which had been lying on the floor being invisibly kicked from a distance of about 12 feet by an unseen force, toward the treadmill at a very fast rate of speed. It crashed against the front of the treadmill, leaving a small crack in the motor cover. It didn't scare me; I was awestruck by the whole experience. However, there is no question in my mind that it was incited by anger.

April 30: One of my roommates was in my bedroom all night. Although I felt its presence and heard a little rustling, I slept pretty well. I had an electrician come out to look at the light outage in the master bathroom. He couldn't readily find what was causing the problem and told me it would take a great deal of effort to find the causation and it would cost me a minimum of $1,565 just to locate the problem. I feel sick about it, but I need get the situation resolved, so I set up an appointment.

I also called my handyman and suggested that maybe he had done something when installing the fluorescent lights in the basement. He said that I was being grossly overcharged and that he knew a master electrician he would like to have come out and look at the situation. He told me he doubted that he had caused the problem, but if that turned out to be case, he would get it fixed at no expense to me.

I still couldn't help feeling that the poltergeist was the culprit. I didn't want to talk to the guilty party directly, but rather talked to myself while doing my housework, lamenting that I didn't have the money to spend on repairs. Later on, my sister called, and I mentioned the problem to her, never once blaming it on the poltergeist...and then my daughter called. As I was talking to her about the financial toll this problem was going to cause me, I walked into the master bathroom, hit the vanity mirror light switch for what I mistook for the overhead lighting, and all the lights above the mirrors went on. I couldn't believe my eyes!

Do I need any more proof that whatever caused this problem has feelings, sympathized with my plight, and repaired the damage? Perhaps it was a ghost! I expressed my happiness to my daughter and went on and on about it. She knew what I was doing. After hanging up, I continued to talk to myself, expressing my relief over the problem seemingly fixing itself. I truly believe this is not a temporary fix, but a permanent one.

Note: In retrospect, I was right!

May 1: It was very quiet last night and today. A light bulb went out among the seven bulbs above the mirrors. It popped when I switched the lights on.

May 2: There was knocking all night! Although it wasn't terribly loud, it was constant and kept me awake.

I've been watching TV, and it went off about five minutes ago. I didn't touch the remote in any way. For whatever reason, it isn't working right now. About a half hour ago, I noticed my computer battery was low. Not sure why; I haven't been using it much.

I've been noticing typing on the computer that seems to happen when I leave it for a time without turning it off. Since this is something new, I believe it's worth mentioning. **It is also happening on my cell phone. So far, just letters and punctuation.**

The TV seems to be working again…oops, I spoke too soon.

May 3: The TV is still being messed with. There was a fair amount of noise last night. It started with three knocks and then other sundry sounds. One of my roomies woke me up this morning, and I wished the pest a "Good Morning." It was a bit insincere on my part…I'm so tired. I just heard three quiet knocks behind me as I type. I wish the knocks would be in any sequence other than three at a time!

May 4: This afternoon as I was reading, I thought I heard organ music coming from the basement. The TV was turned down, and when I turned it off so as to hear the music better, it ceased. The TV was on the Headline News channel where they were discussing a court case…organ music was not involved. I don't own an organ, but it could have been the boombox.

May 5: Another noisy night. I felt the circular pain on my wrist. I didn't get much sleep.

May 6: Typical racket.

May 9: Very quiet day. One of those days that makes me wonder if there is still a haunting going on.

May 10: Very bad night. There was knocking all night. **This thing obviously knows when I use earplugs because in addition to the nudging, the knocking now gets closer and louder. I got up at 9:30 A.M. The pest followed me around most of the day and continued its up close and personal noise.**

I continue to find letters, one or two at a time, that show up in the text area of my phone as well as in my journal writing on the computer. It happens frequently.

May 11: It was quiet last night. I got up about 7:30 and heard knocking. It was very faint and seemed to be coming from the basement.

May 12: I turned on my recorder when I went to bed and left it on all night. The racket didn't stop. There were a number of big "bangs."

May 13: One of the bulbs in the master bathroom above the mirror went out just before I went to bed.

May 15: I slept all right last night. I haven't heard anything yet this morning...okay, I just heard a tap. I've been using the silent treatment for a few days in an attempt to quiet things down. Lately I've been hearing brief static electricity sounds near the bedroom TV. However, as soon as I decided that it was just coincidental, there were two knocks in the same area. This is a little communication skill one of my freeloaders uses when I seem to doubt or ignore its talent. Kind of like its signature when I don't give credit where credit is due.

May 18: It has been a quiet day. The lighting on each side of the garage door isn't working.

I had a friend over, and he stayed until about 1:30 A.M. While he was here, we both heard a noise, and he was the one to mention it. He immediately tried to give what he thought was a logical explanation for it: the house was settling, or maybe it was a raccoon. When I woke up this morning, I heard the same noise again followed by two knocks...case solved!

May 20: Now it seems that the TV in the family room, as well as the one in the master bedroom, is making the static electricity sounds. I'm also hearing a loud cracking noise from both of them. This noise can take place whether they are on or off.

I came home from a walk and noticed that the door leading into the basement was open; that's unusual. I thought of going downstairs to close it but changed my mind. I called my daughter, and she told me that my grandson is having some significant problems in his life. I became somewhat emotional after I hung up. I decided to head out to see my daughter and noticed the basement door was now closed.

I have six pairs of reading glasses, and they are all missing.

May 22: It has been quiet for the past couple days.

May 23: I woke up around 7:00 A.M. and the knocking started. It went on for a good half hour.

May 24: I've been having some doubts about myself and what's going on, so I asked for a confirmation knock and received an immediate response.

May 25: Fairly noisy, but not obnoxious.

May 26: I heard racket off and on in my bedroom last night. It picked up at 7:00 A.M. when I got up but wasn't persistent.

May 27: There was something in my bedroom with me before I went to sleep.

May 31: It has been quiet since the 28th. I decided to leave the recorder on while I was gone today. I listened to it when I returned and heard what sounded like furniture moving…a noise that I haven't heard for a while. I also heard a couple knocks and then the electrical sound from the TV.

I continue to have things go missing and showing up later in odd or obvious places I have already looked.

An eerie thing happened last night. I decided to try out a new small hearing amplifier that fits in my ear like a Bluetooth device. I experimented with it for approximately an hour. Then, just as I was about to doze off, I heard a jolting, loud knock right next to me. A few minutes later, the battery in my amplifier went dead.

June 1: One of the chandelier bulbs went out about 11:00 tonight.

June 2: My son came over, and I asked him to change the chandelier bulb and one above the master bathroom mirror that has been out for a while. He changed them, and they were working. Later on, the same bulb in the bathroom went out again. There may be something wrong with the light socket; it's kind of difficult to screw the light bulb in and out. I replaced it, but when I turned on the chandelier in the master bedroom, another bulb had gone out. I replaced it and now, hopefully, I'll be done with it for a while!

Two of my grandchildren were here. I went down to the basement for something, and they followed me. My granddaughter was interested in the crawl space and asked me to open the small entry door so she could see inside. I was concerned about it, because although I often open it for various reasons, I felt that my roommate wouldn't appreciate my opening it up to anyone else. I opened it anyway, switched on the light, let her see inside, and then locked it back up. They left, and I went to my daughter's house. I was there for just a short time when I received a call from my security company; my house alarm had gone off. I needed to get home because the police were on their way to check things out.

Supposedly, the motion sensor in the basement had set it off. There was no reason they could find for the incident. The sensor is in a corner about four feet from the entrance into the crawl space, and the door was locked, just as I had left it. It's a little too coincidental for me to believe that one of my disgruntled freeloaders had nothing to do with it.

My friend came over in the evening, and while we were watching a movie in the master bedroom, we both heard the clinking glass sound. It happened twice. Then there was a loud crashing sound in the family room.

June 3: Very active.

June 5: My friend stayed the night. He got up around 2:00 A.M., and it sounded as though he had tripped. He called me, and I quickly walked toward the sound of his voice. He was standing in the foyer area, where a significant portion of a large, decorative area rug I keep there, had been pulled back as if to trip him. He chuckled a bit and then asked if I had pulled it back. I think he already knew the answer but wanted to share his experience. Thank goodness he has a sense of humor; moreover, I'm glad he wasn't hurt. This is a bit on the malicious side of the spectrum!

June 9: I've been thinking about the area rug incident and wondering if my friend was playing a trick on me. Maybe he pulled the rug back. I shouldn't think that. He's very honest, and I don't know why I'm doubting him. There have been plenty of malicious things that have gone on in this house. It's just that they have never been directed at anyone but me.

There was a lot of noise in the office today as I was taking care of a few of my bills. The noise wasn't particularly loud, but I could hear it clearly because it was near me...subtle taps, bumps, and a few knocks.

June 10: Last night was very quiet...wonderful! There is something I've been meaning to mention. Since my friend's rug incident a few days ago and my thinking he could possibly have been playing a trick on me, I have found another rug with a corner folded back. I no longer doubt my friend. I don't believe I vocalized my doubts about this situation. Maybe I did over the phone and have forgotten. However, it isn't the first time I've felt like I have no privacy...not in my house or my mind.

June 16: This morning while getting ready to shower, I noticed a long scratch on my shoulder. I didn't feel it happen, but it resembled one I received on my forehead a while back. I'm trying not to respond to a lot of the activity around here, and I think that is a point of contention between at least one of my roommates and myself. Anyway, I asked about the scratch, and I thought I heard a faint knock but wasn't sure. I asked if it was angry with me, and I once again heard what I thought was a very light knock but wasn't certain. One thing was for sure, I felt an evil presence. I mentioned my uncertainty as to whether I had heard the knock or not, and within seconds I heard a crash which literally shook the house. It kind of cracked me up, but I didn't laugh. I then told the body scratcher it needed to stop that kind of behavior. I jest, but I felt something wicked and harmful.

June 19: Interesting night. I decided to open my bedroom windows to let in some cool night air. As mentioned before, my alarm system is disabled when windows are open, but I decided to live dangerously. I hit the hay about 12:30 A.M., turned off the TV, and settled down for the night. About 10 minutes later, I heard what sounded like six knocks: Knock, knock, knock, knock (short pause), knock, knock, but it sounded as if it was coming from outside, and that scared me! Thinking the knocks may have come from a human made my skin crawl, so I closed and locked the bedroom windows and set the alarm. I got up this morning and noticed that one of the bedroom windows was open and the alarm was off.

June 22: I spent a couple days with my daughter due to her gall bladder surgery. I'm back home and haven't heard anything, but I had an interesting experience. My friend texted me and mentioned that he and a woman he has been dating decided to call it quits. I sent a reply expressing my condolences. A few minutes later, I looked at my phone and it appeared that another text was sent. It said "ov guy by." It certainly fits the situation, but I didn't write it OR send it off. I think it meant "Over guy, bye." Unfortunately, my friend had already read it and asked me what I meant. I told him I had no idea where that text had come from and changed the subject. Could this entity be a jealous ghost? I'm beginning to wonder. This is the first time something that made some sense has been typed out. The fact that it was sent is also a first...this is disturbing.

June 23: I went out to the garage to grab something. As I headed for the door into the house, I heard a bang behind me. A mini trampoline, which had been leaning up against the shelving for months, tipped and landed in a standing position; i.e., all feet on the floor. This is the fourth incident like this that has happened in the garage.

July 5: It has been quiet for a few days. I hear noises here and there; they are quiet but distinct.

July 20: It's interesting. Things seem to have slowed down again. While talking with my sister over the phone, I told her that it almost seems like there's nothing here anymore. I'm thinking one of my boarders heard me, because during the call I started hearing a beeping sound in the kitchen where I had been working. Not a new experience, but I checked everything that beeps in the kitchen, and it turned out to be the dishwasher. It does that when it's running and something happens to stop it mid-cycle. Not sure what interrupted the cycle. It's the timing of the whole thing that makes it interesting. Since that call, the activity has become more pronounced.

I haven't been keeping up with my journaling as well as I should, so I'm going to randomly write a few things down: I need to mention that I've been going through a med change. In 2005, after my diagnosis, I was put on oxcarbazepine. It started causing me problems, so in 2008 I was given lamotrigine instead. They are both anticonvulsants. I've also taken zolpidem for sleep and lorazepam at especially difficult times, for anxiety. The doctor has now taken me off the lamotrigine, and today is my first day without psych meds since July of 2005. He doesn't think it's going to be a problem, and I will get together with him to compare notes in August.

Yesterday I was talking to my childhood friend on the landline. The phone was cutting out, and she couldn't understand me. This happens frequently with the three people that I talk to the most...my daughter, my sister, and my childhood friend.

July 21: I was awake most of the night...I think I slept about two and a half hours. Although there was activity throughout, it was low key. I think being off the meds may have contributed to my lack of sleep.

I've been experiencing cold chills today. I was doing some cleaning in the basement and felt the cellar dweller around me. **I felt pressure on the sides of my head a few times.**

My blow dryer went missing again today. Last time it disappeared, I found it on a difficult-to-reach closet shelf. This time I found it stuffed in the back of one of the drawers in my master bathroom. I use my blow dryer every day with few exceptions. For me to put it in either of those places seems unlikely.

I turned on the digital recorder before I left the house this afternoon, and it picked up a lot of noise. **I don't know why I haven't mentioned the sound of kitchen cupboards and drawers opening and closing before.** This is a sound that I hear frequently, and it comes through on my recordings as well.

July 31: I did a recording last night for a couple hours. There were noises throughout the night...some in my bedroom where the recorder was, and others from a distance. **This morning, on my first trip to the bathroom, I noticed a corner of one of the bathroom rugs was pulled back.**

August 1: The activity is around me. It is shadowing me, tapping, knocking, etc. **I saw my psychopharmacologist today...I'm doing fine without the meds.**

August 5: I was working in my office and decided to try taking some pictures of myself using my new computer. Since I could hear and feel something literally bouncing off the walls, tapping, knocking, and carrying on, I invited it to get in the pictures with me. Have I mentioned lately that I'm a complete moron? That aside, I took a bunch of pictures, one after the other, and looked through them after the fact, to choose the ones I wanted to keep. There are a few of them in a row where a dark mass starts to form around my neck and up the side of my face.

Note: I have shared these pictures with others and have received various opinions. Some feel that the dark mass is caused from the lighting in my office. Others think it is a legitimate dark mass. Honestly, I don't know. You decide.

August 14: It has been noisy today, louder than usual and mostly in the basement. I heard what sounded like a hammer banging on one of the steel beams.

I recently did a nighttime recording. Upon listening to it, I determined that I'm experiencing a lot of interruptions during my sleep; there was a lot of noise going on. Based on this finding, I used my earplugs last night and feel more rested this morning. I've been through this process before. I need to keep tabs on my sleeping due to going off my psych meds and some problems I'm having with my left rotator cuff. Although these things could be a portion of the problem, after listening to the recording, I believe the noise is still the biggest deterrent to a good night's sleep.

August 18: While lying in bed this morning, I was given a significant push or kick to the back. It wasn't painful nor did it scare me, but it was very real...as if there was someone behind me in bed performing the act.

This evening, right around 5:30 as I was leaving for my son's house, I decided to set up my computer to do a recording in the basement. As I slowly backed away to check its placement, it started moving...on its own! It turned at an easily detectable pace, for about 12 seconds, and then continued, ever so slowly, as I left the basement. It stopped after a total of 45 seconds of movement, as if it was where someone or something else wanted it to be. In a way, whatever this is seemed to be playing with me and acting out for the camera. On the other hand, it could have been letting me know that I was not the one in control! Unusual behavior for the generally camera-shy boogeyman! Surprisingly, the rest of the video is uneventful. Perhaps it took all of this anomaly's energy to move the computer; or it decided to continue its activity in another part of the house.

August 28: This morning I noticed a kitchen rug with a corner pulled back...it's still happening!

August 29: It was a quiet morning. I had one of my little grandsons over later in the day, and when his mom came to pick him up, there was a noticeable bang in the family room. She looked in the direction of the noise but didn't say anything, and I'm not asking!

I set up my computer in the master bedroom to do some recording while I was gone earlier this evening. I haven't viewed it yet.

August 30: I watched my video today, and I was able to view an orb flying around my bedroom right after I set my house alarm. This is the best orb video yet!

When I got out of bed this morning, I noticed that the dining room light was on. It's hard to believe that I left it on last night, because I would have noticed it from my bedroom. I went downstairs a little later, and the crawl space light was on, which makes no sense. Tonight, when I went to turn on my security system, it was indicating a window in the basement was open…it wasn't. I had someone from the security company come to my house to check my system…they say it is not faulty in any way.

September 5: I couldn't sleep last night. It was a night where I was antsy, tossing and turning, unable to find a comfortable position. I was awake until approximately 4:30 this morning, and during that time I heard a lot of subtle, familiar sounds and a couple big knocks when the intruder seemed to think I was asleep. I also heard an owl outside the master bathroom window along with some muffled voices.

September 6: Today I watched a video I recorded in my bedroom a few days ago while I was downstairs. There's a fair amount of noise, but then, out of the blue, I heard a scary, raspy, incoherent voice. I've never heard anything like it. I can't label it as evil. Although it frightened me, I can't help thinking that it could have been a ghost attempting to communicate but unable to do so.

Tonight, I noticed a corner of one of the bathroom rugs is turned back.

September 7: I was in the guest room doing some things and decided to check my cell phone. It indicated that I had a phone message. I listened to it, and it was the same raspy voice I heard on the video yesterday…I have no idea how to even begin to explain this!

For the past couple of months, my back yard has been taken over by rabbits. This influx has been going on for a while but has grown in numbers…sometimes as many as 15 of them raiding my property at a time! My once beautiful, green, well-manicured yard has been reduced to an embarrassing eyesore. I tried shooing these critters away, filled in my split rail fence with wire fencing which extends to the ground, hooked up a motion activated sprinkler to deter them, and even spread coyote urine around the perimeter of the fence, all to no avail. This situation has caused me undue stress, anger, and frustration.

The owl was outside the bathroom window again last night, and its hooting reminded me of an incident that happened recently. My security system had shown that particular window as open; it wasn't, but as I was checking it, I noticed two dead rabbits outside. They were placed next to each other on a diagonal; one without a head, and the other fully intact, both with their back legs crossed. They were located at the corner of the fence that divides my property from the neighbors. Their legs were pointing toward the bathroom window. They had not been there long, since the blood was fresh and I noticed no decay or flies. Perhaps the owl had something to do with it; however, the placement and timing of my finding them seemed strange. It seemed that I was drawn there by something that knew how to manipulate my security system...especially since the window was not open as indicated.

When I saw the two dead rabbits, I felt a sense of horror and then the thought, "I can get rid of these pests for you, all you need to do is ask..." came to my mind. This was not a higher being offering His services, but I felt it was a demon letting me know that it would be glad to do my bidding, not just regarding the rabbits, but in other ways...all I need do is ask.

This incident stopped me dead in my tracks and has changed my life. I went outside and scooped up the two victims of my anger and hatred and disposed of their frail young bodies, feeling responsible for their demise. Until the damage to my backyard, I had always loved these little creatures and enjoyed having them as pets in my childhood. Seeing them butchered by my father had been devastating.

That was the end of my ranting and ill will toward them, and this memory has served as a red flag when I feel such venom toward any living thing. The realization that this demonic entity believed it had the ability to take me down to a level that low shook me to my core.

September 8: Very noisy last night.

September 17: I continue to hear various sounds that seem to be coming from the bedroom chandelier. Tonight, it sounds like an ice cube being dropped into a glass of lukewarm water. At one time, I thought that the crackling sound like ice being placed in lukewarm water, might be coming from the heat of the light bulbs heating up the plastic façade crystals on the chandelier, but the lights are turned off. I'm also hearing knocks that go from corner to corner in my bedroom.

I forgot to mention that the smoke alarm in the basement started chirping a couple days ago. I changed the battery, but I'm not sure I did it right since it started chirping again early this morning. Maybe the replacement battery is bad, I'll try another one.

September 20: Some knocking in the family room last night and noise throughout the day. I changed the battery in the smoke detector, and it isn't chirping anymore!

October 3: My sister has been staying with me, and although she has been hearing some noises, she always finds what she thinks are practical reasons for them. She was a bit flippant with me, and I did something I shouldn't have done. I told what I consider the trickster to feel free to give her some subtle, benign proof of its existence before she leaves.

Being the amazing house guest my sister is, she had laundered the bedding for the guest bed and was remaking it for the next visitor before her departure. As she was shaking one of the pillows into its case, she heard a bell ring; this would happen each time she shook the pillow into its case. She would pull the pillow out of its case in an attempt to find the bell, but was never able to find one. This happened with both pillows, and was something she couldn't explain away.

After she left, I had a moment in the guest bedroom where I shed a few tears over her leaving. At that point, there was a lot of activity that sounded as though someone was running around the room bumping into walls…stressed like.

October 4: I woke up to light, rhythmic knocking. It wasn't scary; it just woke me up. This is the anniversary of my mother's death.

October 5: There is a lot of noise tonight. I'm thinking I won't be getting much sleep.

October 6: Because I've been hearing what sounds like footsteps and other noises coming from the attic, I did a recording in that area today. Afterwards, I listened to four hours of bumping, whacking, knocking, etc., and it was almost non-stop! During the last hour of the recording, I heard what sounded like one of the neighbor kids throwing a temper tantrum, at which time the noise in the attic became more frequent and louder.

October 7: The rhythmic knocking has been going on each morning since October 4.

October 14: I've been housesitting for my daughter since October 10. I've barely had time to go through the mail and do the little things that need to be done at home. Today the first thing I noticed as I drove up to the house was a dead bullfrog lying in the center of my driveway curb. It looked as though it had been squashed by a car driving over it. It was six-to-eight inches long and hadn't been dead for long. I parked the car in the garage, grabbed a dustpan to scoop it up, and disposed of it.

Anyway, things have been quiet at home. I haven't spent more than about 45 minutes per visit. My daughter's house is much quieter than mine!

October 15: My house alarm went off at 3:10 P.M. No logical reason for it!

October 22: This is my first night home since October 10.

October 23: Last night was noisy. I shut my bathroom and bedroom doors in an attempt to shut out some of the noise, but things just got louder.

It's 11:55 P.M., and I can tell it's going to be another noisy night.

November 6: I've been losing a lot of my journal entries lately. I'm not sure why. However, I had another rotator cuff surgery October 31 and have been taking Percocet...maybe that's the reason.

November 12: I was awakened with a start sometime in the night when I heard two loud bangs. I didn't hear much noise after that.

November 21: A worker was over today to finish up some work he has been doing on the front door. I had him paint it black and install a new doorknob and handle. When he finished his work, I walked him to the door, opened it, and closed it behind him. I then decided I wanted to take another look at the outside of the door, but it wouldn't open. It felt like I was trying to open a part of the wall; the door wouldn't budge. I went outside through the garage to see if I could open it from the outside, and that didn't work either.

The worker hadn't left yet, so I had him try to open it from both directions...even he couldn't open it. He said he would look at it again tomorrow since he is planning on coming back to do some additional repairs. He wasn't feeling well. While spending time in my home, he had become unduly exhausted and dizzy and kept needing to sit down between tasks. I don't know. Maybe one of my roomies doesn't want him to come back.

A little while later, I decided to go out to the mailbox. Forgetting the problem with the front door, I turned the doorknob, and it opened without a hitch!

November 22: The same worker that was over yesterday came back today to patch up my ceiling where I had previously experienced a roof leak. It seemed to be a much quieter day than usual, but that's usually the way it is when someone is over. Then later, as I was getting ready for bed, I couldn't help but notice a whole lot of noise coming from the attic. All I can say is that it sounded like a temper tantrum without a voice going on up there! Maybe the attic occupant is angry over the ceiling patch!

Note: It seems to me that some entities prefer to stay in areas in a house where the corporeal don't spend a lot of time. Attics, along with basements, crawl spaces, furnace rooms, etc., would be some of those places. I tend to believe this could be the case for ghosts in particular. Perhaps they get frustrated when "their" space becomes subject to the living, and that is the reason for some of the noise I heard in the attic.

November 26: It hasn't been as noisy as usual lately. A lot of things are being misplaced, and electrical devices are being unplugged or plugged into different sockets. I am paying a lot more attention to where I put things and my movements throughout the day.

The last couple days have been "scary quiet!" It reminds me of when my children were little; when things got quiet, I figured they were up to something!

For the second time, recently, I heard the house alarm beep as if someone opened one of the entrances to the house. It happened between 5:00 and 5:05 P.M. I checked the doors on both occasions, and they were all locked and bolted.

The other night, I was setting the house alarm just before going to bed, as I almost always do, and couldn't get it to work. I noticed a message on the alarm pad telling me there was a window open. I went all around the house looking for an open window, and they were all locked. When I came back to the alarm pad to attempt setting it again, the previous message was no longer there, and there was no problem setting it.

November 29: My main digital recorder has been missing for at least a month. I decided to look for it in earnest today and found it in my office. It was neatly placed on the front of the desk where it would be hard to miss. I'd been in the office a number of times in my search…it wasn't anywhere on my desk.

December 3: There is no question that last night while I was sitting in my oversized chair in the family room, it was jolted as if it had been kicked. It's my mother's birthday, but I don't think she had anything to do with it.

December 4: I saw a black amorphous shape on my bedroom ceiling about 12:30 A.M. The lights were all out, and I was trying to go to sleep. It didn't move; it was just there. I stared at it, trying not to believe what I was seeing, but this has happened before. I got up, turned on the light, and could no longer see it. I turned the light back off, and it didn't re-appear.

December 9: I saw the amorphous shape again last night. This time it was like a dark cloud...like the darkness had gathered into a common area and just hung there. It isn't that the rest of the room wasn't dark, it's just that the area above my bed showed up as darker. I got up and retrieved my cell phone in hopes of capturing a picture of it, but when I returned to bed, it was gone. At least I know how to get rid of it!

December 12: I saw an orb in the entry today as I was talking on the phone with my sister. I tried to debunk it but couldn't. It came from the front door and went down the basement stairs. I've been seeing an influx of orbs in my house recently; the noise has lessened.

December 17: Things are feeling different. I've been dreaming more often, and because there is not as much noise, I've been sleeping better.

December 18: I heard knocking, furniture moving, etc., but not as much or as loud as in the past. I got up about 8:15 this morning and started my coffee. I went back to my bedroom and heard something drop on the kitchen floor. When my coffee was ready, I went back into the kitchen and noticed a single ice cube lying on the floor in front of the refrigerator. It's not any big occur-rence, and I can't chalk it up to anything paranormal...it's easy to debunk. However, looking at it from the other side, the timing is interesting. I hadn't messed with the refrigerator or freezer since about 9:00 last night. It was easy to hear when it dropped to the floor and difficult to miss when I entered the kitchen...impeccable timing. It is simply one of those things that may be added to others. I'm not putting a lot of stock in it, just noticing it.

December 19: I have a bag of potatoes sitting on a stool in the kitchen. It has been there for a couple days. While I was standing with my back turned to it, and about a foot away, a single potato landed on the floor behind me. The bag was not tipped, and the rest of the potatoes were all snug in the bag when I turned to look at it. Once again, the timing of the incident is what interests me. The usual noise continues, but still not as frequent.

December 22: Today I was pulling an extension cord out from under the bed to remove one of the plugs. As I pulled on it, I felt it jerk back... that's a new one! While I was typing today, it sounded like someone was tapping on a glass with their fingernails. That isn't an uncommon sound, but it would tap and then wait about 15–20 seconds and then tap again... this happened four times.

Later, I was on the treadmill talking to my sister on the phone, and as I was thinking of ending my walk, the treadmill stopped on its own. It was still plugged in, and everything else was running as usual. There was no power outage, and I had no problem turning it back on.

I'm not sure how well I'm sleeping. I'm awakened periodically by knocking and tapping in the family room area; however, I seem to be able to go back to sleep. Also, as I'm sitting in bed typing, I've noticed the lamp light dim as if something passed by it a couple times.

CHAPTER ELEVEN

2014

January 1: I forgot to mention that I explored the crawl space a few days ago because there seems to be quite a bit of noise coming from that area again. There was nothing worth noting. When I went back upstairs into the master bathroom, one of the light bulbs had burned out.

Today, I decided to do a video in the garage because I've recently heard quite a bit of noise coming from that area. The video didn't show movement but picked up a lot of noise. Another light bulb has gone out over the mirrors in the master bathroom.

January 3: Interesting happenings in the garage. I did another recording there and, as has generally been the case, nothing actually moves in the video. It just sounds like it. Toward the end of the recording, things pick up as if whatever is making the noise is trying to draw attention to itself. Then a dog starts barking just outside the garage door, and the noise escalates as if to agitate the dog. This little exchange goes on for approximately two minutes. There is no doubt that whatever is in there is not a dog lover!

I believe the dog was being walked, because people don't generally let their dogs loose in this neighborhood. It made me wonder if the noise in the garage could be the reason for what I feel has been a negative vibe I've been getting from the neighbors recently. I've thought that I'm just

being paranoid, but maybe not. If people are walking by my house and hearing the deliberate, disruptive, racket that I heard on my recording, they've got to wonder what kind of lunatic is living here. I honestly have no idea how long this has been going on.

January 5: I was awakened at 1:00 A.M. by a beeping sound. I don't know where it came from. I went back to sleep and slept quite well.

January 6: Again, I was awakened at 1:00 A.M. I didn't hear the beeping this time though.

I placed my digital recorder in the garage at about 3:50 P.M., just before leaving the house. I listened to it when I returned, and there was a whole lot of noise...especially just outside the garage door. It's kid noise and a dog barking, etc. The most informative part of the recording is where I hear a little boy say: "Did you hear that?!" What followed was quite a ruckus... children yelling, pounding on the garage door, and noises continuing from inside the garage. It was as if the youngsters had heard noises coming from this area before and were trying to provoke whatever was causing the racket. I don't know this for sure...just what it sounded like.

I did another recording in the garage a few days later. I started it at about 5:00 A.M., went back to bed, and stopped it at about 8:15 when I got up for the day. In that recording, I hear a lot of chaos in the garage and then an angry male voice from outside say, "God damn it, lady, STOP!!!" I think I have enough evidence to support the possibility that my neighbors have been privy to this racket for a while.

I've been in touch with my paranormal investigators. I've been depressed, and I'm hoping they can get rid of what is in my garage! I've been getting my recordings and videos organized and ready to share with them. I need to get things under some kind of control. If the neighbors are hearing this racket, they must think that I derive some pleasure from agitating their dogs and children. I'm not sure of this theory, but it's not like I can go to my neighbors and ask them about it. I already feel like an outcast in this neighborhood.

Note: In retrospect, I can't help wondering if this was at least in part the reason for the diminished activity in the house. Perhaps one of the entities had found a new play area or was deliberately causing a fallout with my neighbors.

It bears mentioning that I have begun meditating and, in addition to praying, asking for help from the spirit world. I have also started doing some writing in a semi-meditative state that I will be referring to as meditative writing. I have control of what I leave myself open to and can stop the process at any time. It is as if I'm taking dictation as I once did as a stenographer for those in this world, but now for some not visible to most in this realm.

I've learned that along with what is negative and dark, there are those in the spiritual realm who are here to help us through life's tragedies and inspire us with guidance and love in all things. This isn't something I have embraced in lieu of prayer or the power of God, but in addition to His guidance and direction. I have become acquainted with those I have learned are often referred to as "spirit guides" through meditation. The more I ask for their help, the more I realize that they are probably the answer to many of my paranormal woes. I don't believe I will ever be free of the hauntings, but I do believe that, with their help, I will receive the answers I need to carry on in my life. I refer to them as "The Good." Most often, these are the entities that speak to me. I always ask for their protection during my meditation and meditative writing.

Note: Briefly, a spirit guide is a good, discarnate entity that acts as a guide or protector to a living, incarnate human being. See Chapter 14 for a more detailed description.

January 14: I was awakened this morning by what sounded like a loud growl above me. My assumption is that it came from the attic. I tried to tell myself it was an airplane, but it was too loud and abrupt. One of the overhead fan lights in the family room went out today.

I've done more recordings in the garage the past couple days, and things have been uneventful. I decided to do a recording today while I took my walk. As I was leaving, I mentioned that I was getting bored with the recordings I've been getting and felt that this could be the last one I do. Once again, an act of idiocy on my part. I knew as the words were coming out of my mouth that it was a mistake. What followed was a very lively recording with loud banging and the usual noise.

I had felt confident that if after my parting words there was no more activity, I would be reassured that whatever was there was gone or on its way out. If that turned out to be the case, I wouldn't need to trouble my friends from the paranormal group and didn't want to waste their time. On the other hand, I was bored and possibly deliberately provoking it. The truth is, as bad as this whole experience has been, I've overcome a lot of the fear that goes along with being haunted and become somewhat consumed by it all…it has become a big part my life. I see that I have a problem.

As I was leaving this evening for my son's birthday party, the toilet started running. I don't mean I flushed the toilet and the chain became entangled. I mean out of the blue it started running AS IF the toilet had just been flushed and the chain was entangled. I took off the tank lid, looked inside, and it appeared as normal. I messed with the chain a little, and it stopped.

January 15: The toilet started running again today…same song, second verse.

I haven't heard from the paranormal investigators I am associated with. I'm very concerned about the garage noise. I sent them an email offering to send information that might better prepare them for a tentative upcoming meeting we have planned.

My daughter invited me along with other family members to dinner. Her husband asked me if there was anything new going on in my life. I told him what I tell most people…the truth. Nothing new…just the same old stuff.

January 29: I finally heard from the parapsychologist from the paranormal group. She told me via voicemail that she has been in touch with a

remote viewer in Alaska who says there is nothing paranormal going on in my home; it's animals, small critters who have found a way to come into my house from the cold, possibly mice, rats, squirrels...and something larger in the garage. She mentioned a cat in the neighborhood which may have found a way in. I couldn't believe my ears! She has been in my home and listened to my recordings...

My house is immaculate, almost to a fault; I even keep my garage and basement neat and orderly. As I have mentioned a few times before, I have a reputable pest control group coming out on a steady basis. I have glue boards in the crawl space, basement, and garage; occasionally they pick up a bug or two. I have had mice in the garage on a few occasions, so in addition to the glue boards, I have bait traps; these are checked by the pest control company each time they come out. Once or twice they have shown some activity, but not recently. I have filled in any gaps between the concrete floor and garage door with steel wool.

The only way a critter can get in is through the open garage door. I am beyond conscientious about keeping it shut. I don't like killing animals, and that includes mice. I am not the trusting sort, and I'm as leery of varmints of the human type as I am of them. I don't leave my doors unlocked or my garage door open unless necessary. I like space...neither the house nor the garage is cluttered. If I had animals in either area, I would notice.

Note: Remote viewing is the practice of using extrasensory perception (ESP) to perceive impressions about a distant or unseen target.

January 30: I placed my digital recorder in the attic at about 12:00 A.M. I left it there for a couple hours and then listened to it to determine if there was activity in that area (I was too frustrated to sleep). I heard a cat meowing. That goes on for about a minute and a half. I must admit, it sounded like it could be in the attic, but how would that happen? Then I heard coyotes and an owl; they sounded just as close, and I know for a fact that they aren't in my attic!

My pest control company came out today. Absolutely NO animals in my house or the garage. No way they're in the walls, no droppings anywhere, and the pest control guy even went up into the attic. Nope, no critters in my humble abode. At least those of this world!

February 1: The parapsychologist called last night and agreed to meet with me but won't be available for a couple weeks. I told her I would meet with her any time.

February 9: The parapsychologist and Catholic priest who have both been here before on separate occasions came by. I shared the evidence I have been gathering for their visit. They set up a recorder in the garage for a time, and after that the priest sprinkled salt and holy water throughout the garage and house. We talked at length, and my friend will get back with me later regarding the recording that was done. It has been very quiet since they left.

February 10: It's still quiet. I haven't heard any noise in the garage since my friend and the priest left. Judging from past experience, whatever entity likes that area is probably just biding its time. The priest asked me to hang the cross that I had taken out of the garage back on the wall...I did.

March 15: Well, a lot has happened. The activity in the garage has stopped since the priest's visit. I think his methods have worked, and he told me that if things get bad again, he will come back. I'm going to keep the cross on the garage wall. People can think what they will.

Another group came out March 8. Great people! What follows is some of the evidence and conclusions the two groups came up with:

Much to the parapsychologist's surprise, the recorder in the garage came up with an electronic voice phenomenon (EVP) in which a female says, "Please talk to me, I need you." It came from 38 minutes of recording while my friend, the priest, and I were in the house.

Note: EVP – (Electronic Voice Phenomenon) Disembodied voices captured on electronic recording devices that are not audible to the human ear.

In addition to the recording, my friend re-evaluated the remote viewer's thinking that the activity in my home is coming from animals. While she was here, she transferred some of my recordings to a flash drive and had a noise expert observe and listen to some of my garage videos. He concluded that the noises on the videos were coming from the computer. Of course, I know better.

I know what computer noise sounds like, and I've not heard anything that sounds like growling, thuds, loud banging, or a garage door being shaken and pounded on. I guess it is speculative as to whether the noise was coming from inside or outside the garage door. I always noted if the wind was blowing or other natural occurrences could have caused the racket. There were times when I'd been on a walk and when I returned, I could momentarily hear the noise coming from within the garage. The noise generally ceased when I was near or entered the area. My friend doesn't live here; her perception of what went on would be different than mine. Her job is to question and look for scientific/psychological answers to paranormal phenomena.

Although I have become weary of her skepticism, she has been here for me through some of my darkest times. I'm very grateful she shared the EVP with me...it's amazing. Regardless of our difference of opinion, I have never doubted her sincerity. I believe the demonic activity in my home has ceased because of her time and efforts on my behalf.

I chose not to pursue the EVP. Much of what I had experienced in the garage up to the point of the female voice pleading, "Please talk to me I need you," was not pleasant and could have been demonic. The pleading voice came just before the Catholic priest went into the garage to rid it of the entity causing the problems. I had to assume the voice was not the plea of a woman wanting to "talk" but the last-ditch efforts of something evil that didn't want to leave the premises.

The other group came twice: once to interview me and decide whether to come back and do a full investigation, and the second time to do the investigation. Their sensitives weren't at the first meeting. They came to the investigation with no knowledge of what had gone on at the interview so as not to have any preconceived notions.

Note: A sensitive is an individual who can detect spirit energy with more awareness than the average person through some or all their senses.

One of them felt a lot of mood swings which she likened to "bipolar." She was probably homing in on me. I was elsewhere in the house when she mentioned her feelings to the other sensitive. It was recorded.

The other sensitive determined that what was haunting me was some random male ghost who told her he bothers me because he can. Once again, she had not been made aware of my history or the attacks, so that was insightful on her part. She said the name, John, came to her mind.

Note: I believe it is important to distinguish between the two types of attacks I experienced. There were the attacks that left me paralyzed, unable to utter a sound, engulfed, choked, weighted down, and unable to breathe. This anomaly would pounce on me with no warning of its upcoming plans. There were also attacks that would happen while I was lying on my side in bed. These attacks were different.

It was almost as if someone had been there before I climbed into bed and had been lying in wait for me. This entity would place his arm around me and felt human. Being startled, I would attempt to pull away, but he would strengthen his hold on me, squeezing me around the waist to the point that I couldn't breathe, and then vanish; however, there is more…

I believe it was the second or third time this ghost attacked me that I told him to let go of me as I tried to jerk myself free. I heard a very human, male voice tell me not to be concerned, he wasn't going to hurt me. I then asked who he was and was told that it didn't matter. He then left my bed without applying the usual vice-like torture I was used to experiencing.

The next time I felt him behind me in bed, I wasn't as leery as before, but I should have been. I had allowed this scoundrel to fool me into thinking he didn't have bad intentions, and he squeezed me harder and longer than in the past. I believe this was probably the "John" the sensitive was referring to. It was a debasing experience for me, but nonetheless could be a cautionary tale for someone else.

Before they left, everyone involved in the investigation and I went down to the basement and turned out the lights. They had tried to record some EVPs, to no avail. Then one of the sensitives suggested that I encourage whatever might be down there to make a noise. I said, "Well, sometimes it whistles." At that point, there were three different noises made, one after the other, that we all heard and were recorded. As I recall, it was nothing scary at all...a clink, like two glasses meeting at the end of a toast, maybe a short whistle, and a bell. Everyone heard it, and it provided a pleasant conclusion to the evening.

It should be mentioned that, although it was inappropriate to have two different groups out so close to one another, it wasn't an intentional act on my part or theirs. I had been trying to get the first group to come out to no avail. In my frustration, I started looking for another team. It was after the initial visit with the second group that the first group came through. I was between a rock and a hard place, and I chose not to tell the second group that I had already had someone else out. Although I was aware that such an event could stifle the efforts of the first group, I felt there was still something else paranormal in the house and couldn't give up the opportunity to accept additional help. The purpose of the first group was to rid my house of something more on a demonic level, which I believe they did. The second group confirmed to me that there was nothing in the garage but still something haunting the house.

There are still paranormal happenings going on here. I heard five very distinct knocks a couple nights ago, and TV's and lights have been on some mornings after being double checked the night before. I did a video and a recording in my bedroom while I went for a walk yesterday. There were definite bangs, bumps, etc. I don't have a problem with it. I'm sleeping better and don't feel the demonic presence I have experienced in the past.

Note: At this point in time, things slowed down, and I deviated somewhat from the journal writing. Being able to go back in time and read what I wrote as these incidents were happening leaves less to the imagination and doesn't leave me room to doubt myself or my experience. It has been an invaluable tool in writing this book, and much of what follows is based on knowledge gained from reading, compiling, and contemplating my experience. Although it could leave one wondering if I'm suffering from delusions, I don't believe I am. It is the repetition of incidents, sometimes seemingly small in the big scheme of things, that have brought me to some of my brightest "light bulb" moments. Sometimes it is the things we work hardest to normalize in our minds that prove to be the most telling...

Chapter Twelve

The Move and The Chaos

I had been thinking of moving for a while but became more serious about it in April of 2014. I didn't like the idea of troubling my boys to help with the yardwork, and the price of getting it done professionally was more than I wanted to pay. My daughter knew of some townhouses that could be a possibility. I felt that from a spiritual standpoint the house was sufficiently cleansed and called my realtor. Toward the end of April, I decided to get the process of selling my house started. Pictures were taken, papers were signed, and I put some money down on a townhouse.

My abode of almost eight years wasn't up for sale yet, but I started packing. Things seemed to be going quite well, but on May 4, things started to change. I'd been hearing the faint sound of bells in the basement for a couple weeks but wasn't bothered by it.

I had taken a late shower and was blow drying my hair when I noticed that the water was on in the sink. I didn't recall turning it on for any reason but shook my head, turned it off, and went on with the daily feat of making myself presentable. My next task was to start a load of laundry, which I did, and as I headed out of the laundry room, I again heard the sound of bells ringing downstairs. I decided to check things out, and as I entered the basement and turned the corner, I couldn't help but notice that a portion of the basement was flooded. I waded to the drain, and it was obviously backed up. I went back upstairs, turned off the washer, and mopped up the mess. It wasn't a small job!

However, because something like this had happened before, I thought the problem would fix itself as it had in the past. I went back upstairs and turned on the washer...no such luck! This time I noticed a large amount of toilet paper at the top of the drain, so I unscrewed the cover and pulled it out, hoping that would solve the problem...it didn't.

I voice-texted my daughter: "I won't be able to make it over this evening as planned. I have a flood in the basement I need to clean up." I proofread the text and instead of "I need to clean up," it read, "I need to clean, ha-ha." I thought it was a little odd that "up" came up as "ha-ha." I was starting to feel an uneasy sense of déjà vu.

I once again mopped the floor and then called the City of Broomfield to have them come out and check the sewer line. They came out right away, checked things from their standpoint, and told me all was well. It was a Sunday evening, so I called a plumbing company and made arrangements for them to come out in the morning.

A man came out and snaked the drain, but he couldn't find a problem. The snake came out clean as a whistle. He said one of his cohorts would come out about noon and video the pipes. His coworker diagnosed it as an "offset in the belly." He said they would need to dig up an area of my yard to fix the problem. The estimate came to a whopping $4450.00, of which they needed half to get started.

My mind wandered back to the first house my husband and I owned. One day the city turned off the water as I was filling the bathtub to bathe my little ones. Their father and I had a short excursion planned, so I decided to forgo the bath and continue our plans for the day. As an afterthought, my husband asked me to check the bathtub faucets to make sure they were turned off, which I did. We came home to a flooded house.

Much of the water had dripped down from the bathroom, where the bathtub faucets were ON, to the basement. Of course, I blamed myself as did my husband for the incident. I chalked it up to my stupidity, feeling that I must have gotten confused somehow and turned the faucets back on. The water in the basement was up to my knees. There were toys, boxes, clothing...so many items leisurely floating on the water's surface seemingly enjoying the ride. It was a terrible time, but we did learn that the drain in the basement didn't work and had it fixed.

The next house was worse. It was a split-level house that had a driveway sloped downward to the garage, which was level with the basement. There was no sidewalk, curb, or gutter from the street, and the garage and basement would frequently become flooded on stormy, wet days. We eventually solved the problem, but it was a constant concern and nightmare situation for me for quite a while. My husband was gone a lot and, of course, those were the times the problem would rear its ugly head!

The home was also located on approximately ¼ of an acre of property with irrigation rights which we shared with our neighbors. We all took turns using the water, and oftentimes the "man of the house" would be gone on our turn, and my efforts would cause all kinds of havoc throughout the neighborhood. I was never able to get the hang of irrigating, and all my cookie plates and heartfelt apologies couldn't make up for my lack of skill as an irrigator. There was a lot of stress to be had there…a lot of physical labor and anxiety for me.

We moved a couple more times before we relocated to Colorado. One of those houses had a comparatively minor problem which involved some seepage coming in through cracks in the concrete basement floors. Although my flooding problems seemed to be a thing of the past, things aren't always what they seem.

Our first Colorado house had a problem with water filling the window wells and leaking through the basement windows on wet, stormy days. Compared to what was in store for us, this was a minor problem.

My husband had been quite successful financially, and we moved into a beautiful, spacious new house in October of 2001. It was something that I had never dreamed would be a possibility for us; to me, it was a mansion. It was custom built, and I set myself up as the interior designer. It was something to behold, and I was very proud of my achievement.

One day, shortly after its completion, my husband and I left the premises to take some family members out for ice cream. When we returned home, we immediately noticed water escaping the house from under the entry door to the garage. I opened the door and was met with a forceful flow of water. We located the turn-off valve and found that the flood was caused by a dishwasher hose popping off its connection. The entire house was affected, with the one exception being the master bedroom, which was located on the top floor. It was the biggest flood nightmare yet. The finished basement was all but destroyed.

It took months of living in areas being separated by plastic tarps and workers invading our home day after day to work on the renovation. Truly catastrophic damage in my mind. I believe this incident is what took me to the yet undiagnosed bipolar mania level that ended my marriage. The stress involved in having my house invaded by strangers on a daily basis, insurance disputes, and other related financial woes took a toll on me. I couldn't sleep and started acting out again in ways indicative of bipolar mania.

Meanwhile, back at the ranch…$4450.00 worth of unanticipated grief! I couldn't help recalling one of the most frightening cartoons I have ever seen: *The Sorcerer's Apprentice* starring Mickey Mouse. The music, *Fantasia*, is spooky enough; but add the dark castle, the flood, and the water toting brooms, and it has all the makings of a true nightmare for me! It seemed, at that moment, a never-ending one. I reluctantly made out a check for half and financed the rest of it.

I wondered if my homeowners insurance might pay for some of the costs. I had experienced two roof leaks while in the Broomfield home, and my insurance had covered both. I called my insurance agent and asked the question. I was told that although the flood itself wouldn't be covered, the yard excavation might. He said he would check with the home office and get back with me. He called back and told me they wouldn't be able to help me out. That was fine. I'd just thought it was worth asking.

Two days later, I received a letter of cancellation from my insurance company. I had been with them for some 40+ years, and NOW they were cancelling me?! All I had done was ask a question. So my front yard was being ripped out, AND I had no homeowners insurance! Great way to sell a house! I was beginning to feel defeated, and the "For Sale" sign wasn't even up yet.

Let's see, the bell was still ringing (literally). What future calamity was it heralding now? A little later, I was looking for something in the cupboard under the kitchen sink and noticed that the bottom of the cupboard was wet and warped. The leak had obviously been there for a while but had recently escalated into a more noticeable problem. I contacted a plumber. The leak under the sink wasn't a simple, inexpensive repair either, but it had to be fixed.

I was still fuming about my insurance being cancelled and spent weeks trying to find homeowners insurance. It seemed like the impossible dream, but I finally found an insurance company that found my house acceptable; however, I had to pay a pretty penny for it.

The first house showing involved a male realtor and his male client. They decided to open the trap door in the floor nearest to the drain/flood area in the basement. They noticed that the tarped ground underneath was wet and reported it to my realtor. I hadn't even thought about needing to clean up that mess! However, I immediately forced myself down the hole, and on my hands and knees with a bunch of old towels, dried the black tarp that covered the ground. I didn't experience anything unusual until I climbed out of the pit back into the basement where I heard three or four jovial knocks. I ignored the parasite, went upstairs, put a batch of towels in the washer, and went to bed.

There was still some paranormal activity in my house, but not near as much. I wasn't home a lot, having spent a couple months housesitting for my daughter, almost a month in Washington state on vacation, and then back again for a week due to the death of a family member. Also, we took a family vacation consisting of a week at the Grand Canyon. There were a lot of days spent in making new house choices, showing the Broomfield home, and banking. There was no more demonic activity thanks to the efforts of the Catholic priest. What was left was what I believed to be the poltergeist and an evil intentioned ghost... but that activity had decreased.

I should mention that the seepage beneath the three childhood pictures I had hung awhile back had lengthened to about eight inches by the time I left. Throughout the months since I first noticed it, I had asked a number of people, those involved in the paranormal as well as painters and friends, if they had any idea what the tacky, gooey substance was; nobody had a clue. It never dried but remained in its gooey, tacky state. In addition to my cleaning efforts, I tried painting over it, but that didn't work either. It continues to be a mystery.

A couple days before I left my Broomfield home, I did one more video. There was very little noise, but I heard the TV go on for a time and then go off just before I got home. The day I left, I expected to hear something…but it was silent. I can't remember ever hearing such silence; it was deafening in a way. I hoped the best for the new owners, and I saw them once a few months after their move. They seemed happy. Hopefully, they don't have the predisposition to the paranormal world that I do.

I moved out of my abode December 1 and stayed in a nice little basement apartment until I moved into my townhouse in March of 2015. However, much to my surprise, a bit of what I had experienced in the Broomfield house followed me there. Nothing serious: a few knocks occasionally and missing items being found in odd places. I tried to debunk the things that went on but couldn't. It didn't bother the rest of the household, and it wasn't bothersome to me. I continued praying and meditating and kept in touch with The Good.

CHAPTER THIRTEEN

The Townhouse

I'm not going to mention every detail of the paranormal/supernatural part of my life in the townhouse. Suffice it to say that since the move in mid-March of 2015 and trusting in The Good, things have changed dramatically. However, there are a few incidents that bear mentioning.

I had been in the townhouse for a couple of days. There was a lot of activity around me; furniture being delivered, TV's being hooked up, etc. Because it had been so busy, when I heard two men conversing downstairs, I wasn't surprised. However, I thought everyone had gone for the day and I needed to know who was down there. As I headed toward the voices, I realized they were coming from the furnace room; but as I placed my hand on the door-knob to enter, just as real as the conversation was, so was the sudden silence. I opened the door, and the furnace room was void of anything human. Perhaps a couple of earthbound spirits who didn't realize their space had been taken up by the living, decided it was time to be on their way. There was no fear on my part. I knew what I had heard, and I wasn't afraid. Unlike my previous experiences, I am certain what I was hearing was not coming from any kind of electronic equipment. I have never heard such distinct disembodied voices.

A few days later, I was walking along the sidewalk outside my townhouse and stopped to visit with a neighbor who had been walking his dog. He was standing on a grassy area a short distance from me to accommodate the dog's needs. We had been talking for approximately five minutes when suddenly, under the sidewalk, right where I was standing, a large gush of water broke loose beneath my feet. It was coming out at about the same force as I've seen damaged fire hydrants surge. Although we had a landscape company that left a lot to be desired and there would be other floods to follow, it was the timing of this one that made an impression on me; my history with floods…right underneath my feet? Memories of floods gone by could not compare to the force and spontaneity of this. It was interesting and worth taking note of given my history.

It was early April when I saw the shadow of a figure in a dark hooded cloak casually float across the south wall of my bedroom. It was a side view and literally gave the impression that it was floating, albeit quickly, across the wall. I was caught off guard but watched for approximately four seconds as the cloaked silhouette made its short journey. I didn't have time to study it but watched as it left the house seemingly through the wall to who knows where. I had never seen a shadow like that before…it happened at night, and my room was dimly lit. Not to be forgotten, I wrote the experience down and didn't think much more of it.

It was a couple weeks after that, around 4:00–5:00 A.M., when I got up to use the bathroom. I went back to bed, and as I turned over on my side, facing the bathroom, I saw the cloaked one, this time not as a shadow but as something much darker, even darker than the night. As cheesy as it sounds, in the background, Rachmaninov's Prelude in C sharp minor was playing. As I was trying to shake myself out of what I thought wasn't real, this apparition pounced on me and, as has always been the case, I was rendered paralyzed, speechless, and unable to breathe. As soon as I had breath and my voice returned, I cursed it and banished it in the name of Jesus Christ.

This little experience has given me a lot of food for thought. I had wondered throughout the years if my attackers were dark figures. I had seen dark figures, and I'd been attacked; however, I had never before seen any of my attackers until then. This incident has given me a better perspective as I attempt to categorize the anomalies I've encountered in my lifetime.

This thing didn't scare me. Even with the background music and the way it presented itself in its gothic hooded cloak, it didn't faze me. It was not fear that caused my paralytic state; nor was it fear that rendered me unable to speak or breathe. This is a power this type of demon has over humans. This is something I have thought for some time, but this most recent experience has added fuel to my fire.

This was the second time eerie music had spontaneously filled my home. Just as in the Broomfield house, it was music I don't own. The only equipment I have in my master bedroom that could be manipulated to play music are my TV and cell phone, and they were both turned off. However, neither has the ability to play music as it was played that night in my bedroom; it would require a high-tech sound system. As odd as this is, and as crazy as I may seem, it nonetheless happened.

On April 21, at approximately 4:25 A.M., I was awakened by a loud thump in my bedroom. I didn't think much of it, until I heard a male voice, very distinct and very real say, "You'll be hearing more!"

It was an afternoon in late May. Although I had completed the "moving in" process for the most part, I had a few boxes stored downstairs that still needed to be emptied. I was using a box cutter that belongs to my daughter, with a neon orange handle. As I completed emptying one box and pulled out another, I realized that the box cutter was missing. I hadn't left the downstairs area of my townhouse, so limited my search to that space. I couldn't find it but knew there were more box cutters in the garage, so left the downstairs family room to retrieve another one.

I returned and started the tedious, seemingly never-ending job of cutting through the tape and folding back the flaps of yet another box. It was filled with carefully wrapped glass and other breakable, fragile items. I was enjoying the process...this was a treasure box of sorts. I had gotten rid of many of my ornamental items in an effort to keep my new residence uncluttered by such dust catchers. The ones I had decided to keep were chosen with a lot of thought and care.

I was surrounded by crumpled newspaper and bubble wrap and was near the bottom of the box when I noticed the box cutter...the one with the neon orange handle that had gone missing, just lying there with my treasures! It is this sort of experience that keeps me attached to the paranormal and supernatural. The evil I can do without, but I would miss the magical. As if to add a cherry to the sundae, a pair of familiar reading glasses were sitting, as if tossed with no care whatsoever, temples open, into the box atop the box cutter. I checked my head and, indeed, the glasses I had been wearing were still there. This added a bit more believability to an almost unbelievable incident.

Occasionally, I will be working around the house and a light or lights will be switched on. I was recently walking by the furnace room and heard a male voice as clearly as before. I was taken aback by it but wasn't in listening mode when I heard it, so didn't make out what was being said. It became silent as soon as there seemed to be a recognition of my awareness. This voice was as audible as the two aforementioned male voices I heard in the same location.

On September 5, early in the morning—not sure of the time—I found myself in what I thought was a horrific nightmare. I was alone in a dark place when suddenly, without warning, I was being angrily pushed into a wall. I could feel the hate and complete negativity of this entity. It was all happening in the black of night; I could see nothing. Then the dream turned into reality. I was flat on my back on my bed being crushed by this demonic entity that had now found it necessary to enter my sleep to catch me unawares in my dream state. These cowardly fiends will stop at nothing in their attempts to strike fear and pain. What these ungodly creatures do not understand is that, although at my awakening and in a state of confusion, they may startle me, as soon as I have my breath, it all goes away. This intruder was no more than a worthless twit to me.

There are so many positives here, but that doesn't have to do so much with the place I live but with the way I live. Prayer, meditation, and asking for help from The Good has made for positive changes.

One experience stands out above the rest. I had heard the buzz around the neighborhood that a neighbor had recently passed away. I had met him and his wife at a neighborhood party a couple years earlier. They were nice people, and I spent most of my time at the party visiting with them. I didn't see them much after that but always acknowledged them with a wave if I noticed them drive by or a kind word if I saw them in the neighborhood.

Because they were well known in the area, I felt that the man's wife probably had plenty of help. It was a couple days before the funeral when I noticed her walking alone along the sidewalk outside my townhouse. As I usually do, I had prayed that morning that if I could be of service to someone, I would be guided in that direction. My wordage was a bit different than usual, though. I asked that if I could be the "answer to someone's prayer," I would be drawn in that direction. I had also spoken to my spirit guides and asked them for the same kind of guidance.

I raced out the door and caught up with her. I expressed my condolences and asked if I could help in any way. She seemed somewhat taken aback by my unexpected, sudden appearance but told me she needed to have someone set up her after-funeral luncheon. I told her I would be glad to do that.

She breathed a sigh of relief and said, "You are an answer to my prayers." I smiled and replied, "And you are an answer to mine."

It was October 30, the day of the funeral, and I was ready to walk out the door to make the short trip to my neighbor's house. I heard five knocks at the door, and as I opened it, a forceful gust of wind blew what felt like a large spider web in my face, and there was nobody in sight. As I was attempting to brush the web from my face, my landline phone rang, my cell phone alerted me to a text, and I realized there was no web on my face. At that point, I instinctively knew that I was in the presence of a ghost. I shut my eyes and listened as my deceased neighbor communicated a message he wanted relayed to his wife. To say I was touched by this experience would be an understatement. I told him I would be glad to share his message.

It bears mentioning that I am very much aware from my experience with the spiritual realm that if I feel like I have come in contact with webs, only to find there aren't any, I may be in the presence of a ghost. When there is a sudden increase in activity, one thing immediately following another, an entity from another realm could be summoning me, and I need to stop and listen. This is only one of many experiences I have had with The Good…synchronicity at its finest. However, this book is about a haunting, and for the most part, I want to stay on course.

What follows is a summary of the paranormal/supernatural entities I believe I have encountered in my life and some personal insights as to my understanding of their abilities and what may or may not distinguish them from one another…the final phase, or anatomical conclusion of my haunting.

Chapter Fourteen

Entities

Ghosts

These are spirits who have remained in this realm after death, often referred to as earthbound spirits. In my humble opinion, there are many ghosts among us. I can't speak for most of them but only surmise through my studies and experience why they may still be here.

There are no definitive answers, only a lot of thought-provoking theories. If seen, they generally appear in spirit form in much the same way as those who have moved on to the next realm; however, some can present themselves in sinister ways to frighten the individual they are appearing to.

There are many dead who were unsavory characters in life who have possibly chosen to stay in this realm to continue the evil acts they manifested here in the flesh. Others may be afraid to move on for fear of the hell they believe awaits them. Whatever characteristics these specters depicted in life, they will likely continue to exhibit in death, generally haunting places and people they were associated with in this world. *In paranormal circles, they are sometimes referred to as evil spirits. In my book, this is the way I use the term. In biblical terminology, they are most often, if not always, synonymous with demons.* At any rate, these unhappy entities can inflict pain and illness on the living and cause feelings of dread, anxiety, and despair. Although they have characteristics similar to those of a demon, they don't have the same strength or ferocity of one.

There are also those who are stuck here in a state of confusion. Perhaps they experienced a death so sudden as the blink of an eye and have not yet recognized their demise. Innocent children and the mentally impaired sometimes fall into this confused state. They may not understand the concept of death and need to be helped on to a better place.

Some have died in tragic ways at the hands of another. They sometimes choose to stay here to reconcile what has happened to them. They may not be at peace because their death has not yet been acknowledged or because their body has not been laid to rest. They might be seeking retribution for dying at the hands of another and/or want to stop the perpetrator from inflicting the same harm on others.

Many are simply attached to what they had in life, whether it be a home, a property, or a person. Often, they are stubborn, mean, selfish, unkind, and inflict all kinds of torture on the corporeal inhabitants who dare to take possession of what they perceive as theirs. Others don't mind the new inhabitants but don't want to go on to the next realm. They stay, not meaning to cause havoc, but generally don't go by completely unnoticed.

Most hauntings are brought on by ghosts, and for those who want to be rid of their resident haunt, there are ways to hopefully achieve this end. It could be that the specter just needs some coaxing to go on to the next world. Those who didn't believe in the concept of life after death in their corporeal state may just need some guidance. If they are mean and stubborn about leaving and are trying to push the living out the door, a blessing or cleansing of one's house could be in order. The worst-case scenario is that an exorcism of the house may be needed. Mediums, clergy, and those involved in paranormal phenomenon are good people to call on for help. On rare occasions, the living may find it necessary to leave.

I believe that what stalked me in the Manchester house was a ghost. The sound of heavy footsteps coming up the stairs was very human-like. Although I don't recall the stalker leaving with the same dramatic flair, I do remember the chuckling I would hear on occasion. It was as one would hear from an incarnate male.

As previously mentioned, I believe the attacker that assaulted me in the Broomfield house while I would be lying on my side was an evil spirit. The most telling sign is the physical nature of these attacks. My attacker felt corporeal and at one point spoke to me in an audible voice. Unlike what I describe as demonic attacks, I was able to fight back and speak or curse at this thug on occasion during the assaults.

I have seen three ghosts. None have been of anyone I've known in life, and they seemed to be completely oblivious of my existence...just passersby seemingly on their way somewhere. I believe I have received messages from a few ghosts through my meditative writing—some negative, and some positive.

Attachments

On more than one occasion, I was described as having a "spirit attachment." Another explanation for this phenomenon is to say that I was haunted, not my surroundings. These entities aren't necessarily someone to whom we are related or have known. A ghost can become attached to an individual simply because they have had a like experience as that person in life. It is the same as when we come across a person in the physical realm with whom we have a lot in common. This can go unrecognized by the victim for an entire lifetime.

The difference between an attachment and a possession is that attachments involve a ghost that has attached itself to a person's aura. *In spiritual terms, the aura is the distinctive atmosphere that surrounds and is generated by a living person...their spiritual essence.* This enables the specter to influence the person, but not to possess them. The affected human is still a free agent. When I speak of possession in this book, it is regarding demonic possession, meaning that a person has been taken over by a devil.

Ghosts don't generally attach themselves to individuals, but those who do are negative in nature and find unhappy, depressed, vulnerable individuals with whom to attach themselves. Their influence can enhance negative behavior, change the personality of their prey, and influence them to do things outside the boundaries of what they would ordinarily do. They can sap one's energy, leaving them tired, weak, and more vulnerable to other evil spirits and the demonic.

During the time of my Broomfield haunting, I took a trip to Washington state and awakened one morning at my first destination (my sister's house), to find fang marks on my ankle. A week later, while staying at my childhood friend's residence, I awakened to find the same sort of marks on my shin. It seemed as though one of my unwelcome tenants was a "bloodsucker" of sorts and had decided to join me on my trip.

Was this leech leaving its "calling card" in the form of fang marks to let me know it had the ability to follow me? Since receiving this type of mark had not been a common occurrence, to have it happen twice in two different locations in the span of two weeks made a definite impression on me...in more ways than one! Both marks were accompanied by fresh, red blood and were noticed in the morning when I awakened. Because the fang marks didn't happen a lot, to note the possibility of this experience being indicative of an attachment seems worthy of consideration.

A well-trained mental therapist can help rid us of such a parasite by giving us the mental tools necessary to better understand and face the negative influences plaguing us. These specters, while being dealt with as an influence versus a paranormal entity, will find they no longer have anything in common with their more positive prey, and leave.

Also, a good psychic medium along with others who are able to communicate with the dead can help. Once understood and confronted, our chances of leaving this vampire behind us and going on with our lives is far greater.

Dark Figures

Bear with me as I provide a brief recap of my visual experiences with dark figures: The first one showed itself in what I refer to as my childhood home shortly after moving in. I was probably five or six years of age. This anomaly made not a sound but would show itself in my bedroom doorway occasionally and presented itself as a Victorian male. It always appeared to me in the same manner.

My second dark figure encounter, and first attacker, manifested many years later. I believe it was in 1992. I would have been 43-44 years of age. Aside from the bumps in the night that never went away completely, I hadn't had any paranormal or "dark figure" experiences that I recall since the dark Victorian man. It was so random and unexpected. Although this scoundrel presented itself in the daylight in what looked like overalls, like the Victorian, it was totally black.

The assault was in the dark and happened several weeks later. I didn't see this fiend during the attack, but given the many years that had passed since having any significant paranormal/supernatural experiences, to relate these two occurrences to each other seems a plausible conclusion.

Then there's the last aggressor, which was seen in my townhouse in mid-April of 2015. In this situation, I can say with 99 percent surety that it was a dark figure that attacked me.

I didn't see any of these anomalies in the Broomfield house. Although I was attacked multiple times and felt the culprit was one, I didn't witness such. Seeing the last dark figure just before it attacked me in my townhouse added credence to what I had always suspected—i.e., that my attackers were dark figures. However, I can't ignore that the Victorian I witnessed in my childhood home, although frightening, never attacked me.

Nothing is set in stone, and as much as I would like to categorize my assailants, the attack I experienced on February 26, 2011, in the morning light, was exerted by something I could not see. Although it was equally frightening and the attacker acted out in a similar manner as past dark assailants, it seems that I should have been able to observe it as with the second dark figure I saw in the daylight. Seeing its movements pushing down on me and the down bedding left me aghast!

A lot has been said about these anomalies. They have been referred to as shadow people, phantoms, shadow ghosts, demons, and others. I can give one general description to the three that I saw. They appeared as dark male humanoid silhouettes. They weren't a mist that turned into a silhouette as some report seeing, but from beginning to end looked like dark human figures. I could see no features. Although some claim to see them in their peripheral vision, I saw all three straight-on. They didn't appear against a structure, but in open spaces, and they were darker than shadows. In the mental health field, something seen in one's peripheral vision is often labeled a "disturbance," which is a mild hallucination. What I saw were not "disturbances," just very disturbing!

From my studies, I have learned that Victorian males with top hats, and hooded, cloaked dark figures specifically, are somewhat common in the realm of "dark figures." The attacks I attribute to them, i.e. pressure on my chest, paralysis, inability to breathe by way of suffocation, choking, or engulfment, were the same as those wielded by unseen, predominantly nighttime attackers in the Broomfield house.

The explanation we get from skeptics and mainstream science—generally, people who have never experienced them—is that they are something pulled out of the human imagination…our minds playing tricks on us. Because these aberrations don't seem to want to be seen, they are often quick to leave our sight at the first sign that they might have an observer. If you are seeing them, document your experience. How often do you see them? What are they wearing? Where and when are you seeing them? Are they attacking you?

It seems a fairly common consensus in the study of the unexplained that they are not necessarily evil. The Victorian seems to fit into this belief system. My conclusion is that they, like so many entities, are still up for debate.

Many who have studied and/or experienced this phenomenon believe them to be ghosts. Like other specters, some have learned to alter their appearance. Like a hunter in the woods wearing camouflage to make themselves blend in, dark figures generally present themselves in the dark, in dark clothing to facilitate an attack, to haunt, or to hide. Like other ghosts who appear in a more conventional way, the kind of ghost they are varies according to the type of humans they were; I see them differently…

Demons

These are hostile, resentful entities of non-human origin; these things are pure evil. You cannot appeal to their better side because there isn't one. Every evil thing that can be attributable to the paranormal, these fiends can do to the "nth" degree! They tempt, scheme, oppress, and can eventually defeat those they target, and they want your soul.

A unique attribute of these creatures is their stench. They are often described as smelling like rotting flesh, rotten eggs, and sulfur. Other smells cannot be described in earthly terms other than to say they are "foul."

Demons are very strong and can maim, possess, or kill their victims. Scratches, bruises, bite marks, and being forcefully pushed, pulled, dragged or thrown, are all warning signs. Scratches that appear as three claw marks are especially concerning, and I have experienced such on a few occasions. Although ghosts can also inflict pain, bite marks, etc., demonic attacks are generally more severe.

Their hauntings can take place at any time, but there is often an increase in activity around 3:00 A.M. There are many theories for this, but suffice it to say, many who study the supernatural agree that this is the time pure evil likes to cause its worst havoc. Also, when you hear loud ungodly noises in threes, this can be a sign of the demonic. Once again, a mocking of the Holy Trinity.

These monsters can influence our dreams with nightmares that often contain violence, dark images, and dark ideas. By interrupting our sleep patterns, we become easy prey to their evil schemes. We're in a vulnerable state when asleep, and a lack of slumber brought on by their merciless torture weakens our senses and can lead to oppression and possession.

Growling sounds are generally attributable to demonic hauntings. Scratching in/on walls, banging, knocking, footsteps—all signs of a ghostly haunting—can be present in a demonic haunting. Once again, it is the intensity that often determines whether one is being haunted by an evil spirit or a demon. Demons possess inhuman strength and can move heavy appliances such as refrigerators and stoves and heavy pieces of furniture such as beds, couches, etc.

Always keep in mind that deception is a demon's greatest tool. They can take many forms, including someone you know, alive or dead, and even that of a child. They can also take on the appearance of your worst nightmare. For those who believe that they have seen them in their true form, seeing them again can be their greatest dread. They are dark, monstrous, and frightening.

Those unfortunate enough to experience possession may show signs such as inhuman strength, and multiple voices may come from the victim at the same time. They often exhibit unusual inhuman movements, dilated pupils, and/or a change in eye color commonly described as black, yellow, or red.

If you are plagued by something like this, don't waste time, it can only get worse. My best advice is to consider an exorcist of some sort. This could be a priest, shaman, demonologist or other specially prepared clergy.

I believe that the two attacks I experienced by dark figures were demonic in nature. I believe the similar attacks, although unseen, were executed by the same. Although I wouldn't say my attacks were necessarily sexual, in that I never felt a phallus, my attackers manifested in much the same way as other victims describe incubus or succubus attacks.

An incubus is defined as a male demon who sexually attacks women; a succubus appears as the female equivalent and attacks men. While some describe their experience with these attackers as salacious, mine were not. These devils stalk, incite fear, and abuse much as a rapist would; control being their primary gratification. Unlike their human counterpart, what makes them different is their ability to paralyze and silence their victims by their very presence. No ropes, chains, duct tape, or blindfolds needed. The suddenness of their presence and departure leaves their victims wondering whether the incident actually happened and leaves them more vulnerable to other like attacks.

Although the attacks I attribute to them were not as brutal as many others have experienced by the demonic, they were brought on by something that reeked of evil. They sometimes seemed robotic in nature, in that they were controlled by something else. However, whether the devil or his minions, it seems these hellions enjoy bringing their victims to the brink of death and then, so they can cause the same havoc again, leave them be to fester in the cesspool of fear they have created, like soaking a piece of meat in a tenderizing brine overnight so as to make it easier to chew on after.

Regardless of who's who in the zoo of the demonic, I allowed these fiends and others into my life by cutting God out of it. I succumbed to the temptations offered me in this world without conscience and with blatant disregard for the possible consequences of my actions.

Poltergeists

Poltergeist is a German word taken from the German verb "poltern," which means to knock, and "geist," the German word for spirit or ghost. The most common definition given to poltergeists is "noisy ghosts." They are wizards of sound and maestros extraordinaire. Those of us who have heard their expertise know there is nothing known to man with which to compare it. Their repertoire is as vast as time immemorial and bows in obedience to their command. They are also tricksters…

Certainly, the "trickster" reputation of poltergeists lends to the idea that poltergeist activity is often brought on by the living; perhaps a mischievous child who likes to hide and throw things, bang on walls, etc., especially if they feel that they are getting attention from and fooling adults. For the record, I use the term "trickster" more in the mythical sense of the word…mischievous, or a magician of sorts.

Claims of poltergeist activity have also been chalked up to psychological factors such as illusions, memory lapses, hallucinations, etc. Certainly, this has all been proven to be true in many situations, but equally true is the idea that these activities can be brought on by something else, unseen and unexplained.

There are many convoluted explanations for poltergeists. If the definition of the word is correct i.e., "noisy ghost," then I cannot leave a poltergeist out of my anatomy of a haunting. However, although I feel poltergeist activity has many similarities to that of a ghost, there are others that I feel make it unique.

Stone throwing, the sound of a deluge of raining pebbles, or "pebble noises" in other forms have been attributable to poltergeists for centuries. They have been accused of being responsible for spontaneous outbreaks of fire where no spark or source of fire existed and on non-flammable surfaces. The escape of articles from closed receptacles without any discernable means of exit and the odd stacking and configuration of objects, both large (such as chairs) and small are classic activities believed to be brought on by poltergeists.

Unexplained puddles and small floods along with electrical problems, especially in homes, are often attributed to them. Also, the disappearance or hiding of domestic odds and ends which are often restored in mysterious ways and in odd places. These types of phenomena have been documented since ancient times and attached to the poltergeist theory for many years.

These are the more classic signs. Many believe them to be ghosts and/or demons, which leaves them open to pretty much all the activity that went on in my house. It is up to the reader to make their own determinations.

I believe them to be supernatural beings versus ghosts, but not evil intentioned as demons. I believe they have been around for ages and that accounts for some of the more archaic sounds such as bell ringing, hotel call bells, clinking of various objects, etc., which I believe they make at will.

Whether or not my flooding problems have been brought on by poltergeist activity, a ghost, or something else is speculative. Since I have only my own experience to draw from, I don't know if what I consider notable flooding problems are such or not. These mishaps in my life could simply be coincidental and are easily explained. It is more the frequency and timing of them that has caused me to take notice. I continue to have plumbing and flooding problems in my townhouse.

Since I tend to believe these anomalies are supernatural, my approach is to give them a second thought as far as some of the damage they can do. It is possible that ill will is not their intent. Empathy is part of the human condition and not something an aberration that has never experienced such a state would be able to relate to in realistic terms. Understanding the magnitude of a flood or electrical problems in a house, along with the ensuing damage physically and financially for one who is corporeal, would be beyond their comprehension. Also, they have an inability to understand time, since time in terms of how it is measured in this realm would probably not be relevant in theirs.

I do believe they are intelligent and have independent qualities one from another. The times I asked that missing items be returned, and they were; other times, when I asked that the noise in my house cease and it did, helped define in my mind what I was dealing with. Although their obedience is generally short term, I once again chalk this up to their possible lack of understanding where time is concerned in this realm. When I was dealing with what I felt was an evil spirit or demon, it seemed there was no stopping them or toning down their activity. In fact, my requests only served to make things worse.

In my experience, no rocks have been thrown at me, no unexplainable fires have materialized; just consistent reminders, beginning in childhood, that there is more to life than just what meets the eye, and that it is not poltergeists, per se, but "phony poltergeists" I need to be wary of.

Often labeled as demonic and evil, I believe they cannot be pigeonholed. They are unique, mysterious, and require far more research. From my perspective, the reason they are confused with demonic or evil entities may be because they are precursors to such. In retrospect, the taps, bell ringing, beeps, and other subtle sounds in "threes" I heard during my Broomfield haunting may have served as warnings of upcoming demonic or other malevolent activity, and were possibly brought on by a poltergeist. I don't believe that demons tap, ring bells, make beeping sounds, etc. They are tormentors; irreverent, cumbersome, loud, undisciplined monsters!

Many believe that ghostly or demonic activity starts out in small, insignificant ways and escalates into a full-blown haunting. Once again, perhaps there are two things going on: the poltergeist heralding the malevolent one's upcoming arrival or attack, and the ensuing, more brutal, frightening actions of an evil spirit or demon.

What I refer to as a poltergeist, while capable of causing havoc in its own way here and there, I believe has never meant me harm. Honestly, you'll probably never hear this philosophy anywhere but here. Another common theory is that their activity is short term. Obviously, that has not been my experience. Once again, I believe that they are often used as patsies for the demonic and confused with ghosts; hence, the answer to my warning so long ago: "Beware of *phony* poltergeists."

I cannot legitimately deny that there is a bit of romanticism involved in my perception of what I refer to as a poltergeist. It stems from some of my earliest recollections of an "invisible friend" of sorts, that although not visible or acknowledged, made me feel less alone as an introverted child. It is the mischievous "trickster" reputation of poltergeists along with their unmatched manipulation of sound and the magic of what this anomaly has added and continues to demonstrate in my life, that leads me to describe it as a poltergeist.

Although I do not believe these entities are evil or demonic, many reputable, experienced paranormal investigators, demonologists, and clergy believe they are. There are many documented cases of poltergeist activity; entire books written about them. There is another aspect to poltergeists that needs to be addressed:

RSPK

Parapsychologist William G. Roll coined the term "recurrent spontaneous psychokinesis" in 1958 to explain poltergeist cases. It is a complicated theory which suggests that poltergeist activity is human rather than spirit based. It implies that an agent, most often a troubled adolescent, in an attempt to relieve themselves of repressed or unresolved emotional stress, unconsciously causes psychokinetic disturbances around them over which they have no control. Scientifically, psychokinesis has not been convincingly demonstrated, and it needs to be noted that, even in severe cases of repressed stress, psychokinesis has not been regarded as a manifestation of such.

A popular belief among paranormal investigators is that some entities, especially ghosts, get their energy from the atmosphere and from humans… especially those going through difficult, emotional times. To note that, and in view of the emotional times pubescent youth go through, it would be easier for me to believe that poltergeists MAY be attracted to them because of the energy they unfurl, rather than to believe that humans create poltergeist activity. However, from my perspective, such a tendency infers that poltergeists are ghosts, which I am not yet ready to believe.

At best, if everything tangible and intangible is energy, concerning the energy we cannot see, we have the ability to feel its emanation in the atmosphere, whether negative or positive. When an intangible form of negative energy becomes dominant, tangible forms of energy can be moved. Whether this is brought on by unseen evil entities doing the background work is up to the perception of the reader. It is the same with positive energy and the beauty and miracles it wields, which can be brought on by the energy itself, or the intervention of that which is good.

While I believe RSPK to be an interesting study, I believe it has nothing to do with poltergeists or poltergeist activity. Although, as the definition implies, this activity is most often brought on by adolescents, it has been suggested that I could be the instigator of such. For the record, I don't buy it. Regardless of your personal philosophy of a poltergeist or RSPK, there is help available.

Consider consulting a mental therapist, especially if you adhere to the RSPK theory and feel that you are a "poltergeist agent" bringing on negative activity. Once again, energy is all around us, both negative and positive, and there is a lot to be said for the effect it has on our lives. Those in the mental health field can be a godsend to anyone suffering from the results of negative, dark energy; addressing mental agony is the crux of what they do, albeit described in different terminology. Also, clergy, a good parapsychologist, and others involved in psychic phenomenon, are good people to get in touch with.

Spirits

These are often deceased friends or family who have passed on to the next realm and are now able to revisit the physical world. These beings can make their presence known through the use of symbols, sounds, and smells that remind us of who they were in human form. They return to offer comfort and understanding in troubled times; many lovingly refer to them as guardian angels. I believe some are spirit guides and/or authors of the meditative writing I've accumulated. If we are fortunate enough to see them, they would seem as they did in life, only in a more perfect, semi-transparent form. They may appear as complete bodies or in part, and sometimes they appear in a foggy mist. They often show themselves in period or familiar dress. Although seeing one could be startling, their intentions are good.

I have seen one in my mind's eye during meditation and have a cherished picture of another taken at the burial site of an aunt. The aforementioned spirit seen in my mind's eye was a male and I believe is one of my spirit guides. He looked as I believe he did in life, perhaps at the age just preceding his death.

He was relaying a message to me that I was able to discern from his movements and lip reading. He seemed to be in his 60's and appeared in casual business attire. He seemed happy and excited to let me know that he had been one of The Good who had recently helped me when I called upon them. He beamed with kindness, and it was wonderful meeting him.

The picture is of my ex-husband's Aunt LaPreal and was taken with a Polaroid camera by his father in the late 1960's at her burial site. Those mourning her loss, including my father-in-law, did not see LaPreal in person, but her image was captured in the picture. This has been a cherished family heirloom for years, and although I realize the skepticism it may incite, I've also seen the comfort it has offered many. It is with that intention that I share it. I don't know if the original picture still exists, but I had some reprints made several years ago. Although they didn't turn out as sharp and well defined as the original, for those who knew her, the white figure to the left is LaPreal in spirit. Imagine my father-in-law as the polaroid print started to develop…I'm sure he was more than taken aback. I'm not sure what his personal belief in the afterlife was, but he never doubted the authenticity of this last picture of his beloved sister.

Spirit Guides

My life has changed significantly since I decided to call on The Good. They are willing to help but don't interfere with my freedom to choose. They want me to be successful in my efforts to live a service-oriented, worthwhile life and keep me in tune with the good I can do. Their use of synchronicity serves as a reminder of their presence in my life and provides me with the guidance and direction I need to be in the right place at the right time.

Our guides may be deceased relatives or other spirits devoted to helping the living from the spiritual realm. I have found the extent of their love, selflessness, and nonjudgmental acceptance of all in this world, far beyond my comprehension. They calm me in times of stress and comfort me in times of sadness and mourning. They are not a part of my life because I am special, but simply because I have asked for their help. They are available to and around all of us, often helping us unawares. Some say there is a reason for everything, and if not for the experiences laid out in this book, I would probably never have known of their existence and been able to reach out to them. Their presence and availability are an undeniable influence and necessity in my life; they are the anatomical silver lining to my haunting.

Signs of A Haunting

I've certainly mentioned a number of them already throughout this book but don't want to leave anything undone. Trying to determine the type(s) of entities we are dealing with in a haunting is confusing because they are typical of each other. Trying to classify a paranormal or supernatural entity is difficult, and hopefully my personal efforts will show you why.

When you look at the following incomplete chart, you will see that the commonalities between entities is obvious. Although I have segregated a few "signs" as specific to various described entities based on the incontestable nature of one over another, they often overlap. For example, the first "sign" listed, "Activity starts up when you attempt to pray," will alert any experienced paranormal researcher or demonologist to the possibility of a demon. However, it is also possible that the activity could be incited by a disgruntled, non-Christian ghost. In an effort to alert the reader to the warning of a demonic attack, I give the demon connection dominance.

Because this book is based on my own personal observations, this chart is also determined, in part, by my individual experience and perception, and is limited to the entities/anomalies I feel are the metaphorical anatomy of my haunting. This is not science...

Signs of a Haunting	Ghosts	Attach-ments	Dark Figures	Demons/ Demonic	Polter-geists	RSPK	Spirits
Activity starts up when you attempt to pray				X			
Air feels heavy and oppressive				X			
Appear in sinister ways	X		X	X			
Appliances being manipulated	X				X	X	
Appliances being moved				X			
Banging	X			X	X	X	
Bells ringing	X				X		
Bites/Bite marks	X			X			
Blinking Lights	X				X	X	X
Bruises, Unexplained	X			X			
Crashing Sounds	X			X	X	X	
Cupboards, doors, and drawers being manipulated	X				X	X	
Cuts and gashes (unexplained on walls, floors, furniture, etc.)	X			X			
Cuts on the flesh	X			X			
Dark black figure			X				
Deceptive	X			X			
Depression, dread, anxiety, and de-spair (uncharacteristic to individual)		X		X			
Diembodied Voices	X						
Electrical Devices being manipulated	X				X	X	

Signs Of A Haunting	Ghosts	Attach-ments	Dark Figures	Demons/ Demonic	Polter-geists	RSPK	Spirits
Electrical Problems	X				X	X	
Electrical Sounds (especially static)	X				X		
Exhaustion	X	X	X	X	X		
Eyes: dilated pupils, change in color (red, yellow, black)				X			
Fang Marks: Paranormal/supernatural possibilities	X	X	X	X			
Fear and Dread	X		X	X			
Feeling of being watched	X		X	X			
Fires	X			X			
Fires (spontaneous, and on non-flammable surfaces)					X		
Floods	X				X		
Footsteps	X						
Furniture being moved seemingly on its own	X			X			
Furniture being moved (sound of), could also be residual					X		
Giggling	X						
Growling				X			
Hair Pulling	X				X		
Hissing				X			
Hitting	X			X			
Hoofbeat				X			

Signs Of A Haunting	Ghosts	Attach-ments	Dark Fig-ures	Demons/Demonic	Polter-geists	RSPK	Spirits
Illness	X	X		X			
Items generally powered by electricity or batteries operating on their own					X	X	
Items (small) moving seemingly on their own	X				X	X	
Knocking	X			X	X	X	
Knocks on doors at odd times and for no reason (nobody is there)	X			X	X	X	
Lights flickering or going on and off seemingly on their own	X				X	X	X
Music coming from an unknown source					X		
Negative changes in personality		X		X			
Nightmares: Vivid, containing violence, dark images, and dark ideas				X			
Nosebleeds, spontaneous and uncharacteristic of subject				X			
Objects disappearing and never being found again	X				X		
Objects disappearing and being found in unlikely locations	X				X		
Objects disappearing and later found where they originally were	X				X		
Objects seemingly kicked or thrown by an unseen force	X			X	X	X	
Odd looking creatures seen in peripheral vision or straight on				X			
Oppression and depression uncharacteristic of victim	X	X					
Odd stacking or placement of items				X	X		
Oppression (prolonged) and possession				X			
Orbs (indicative of)	X		X	X			X

Signs Of A Haunting	Ghosts	Attachments	Dark Figures	Demons/Demonic	Poltergeists	RSPK	Spirits
Pebbles: the sound of pebbles being rattled, dropped singly or in large masses					X		
Physical Harm (unexplained physical manifestation)	X		X	X			
Pinches	X						
Puddles and Small Floods (generally in homes or other structures)	X				X		
Pulling, pushing, and hurling humans (forcefully)				X			
Pulling and pushing humans	X			X			
Pushing downstairs or tripping	X			X			
Religious objects being destroyed or desecrated				X			
Retaliation at an attempt to stop paranormal activity	X			X			
Scratches (on walls, floors, furniture, etc.)	X			X			
Scratches on the flesh	X			X			
Scratches on flesh (3-claw)				X			
Scratching Sounds	X			X	X		
Sexual Assaults	X		X	X			
Slams	X			X	X	X	
Slaps	X			X			
Smell of rotten flesh, meat, or sulfur				X			
Smell of tobacco, perfume, or other scents possibly attributable to corporeal life	X						X
Stomping				X			

Anatomy of a Haunting

Signs Of A Haunting	Ghosts	Attach-ments	Dark Figures	Demons/ Demonic	Polter-geists	RSPK	Spirits
Stone throwing	X				X	X	
Tapping	X				X	X	
Temperature changes, sudden and generally cold in a specific area or affecting a specific person	X						
Threes: Loud knocks, pounding, bangs, etc., done 3 times, and activity at its peak around 3:00 a.m.				X			
Threes: Subtle sounds like taps, bell ringing, beeps, etc. done three times					X		
Tricksters (magicians)					X		
Unseen (as in invisible as opposed to having the ability to show itself)					X	X	
Unusual, inhuman movements				X			
Vomiting, sudden and unexplained				X			
Webs (Feeling of walking through)	X						
Wind or breeze coming from no logical source; especially within a building	X						X

Further Explanations

Attachments are in fact ghosts and, therefore, the signs of ghost hauntings listed on the chart could apply to them as well as those that are more specific to them. I give them space and separate them because I don't believe that most ghosts attach themselves to the living, and this makes them somewhat unique.

From my perspective, dark figures are typically demonic. They stalk and attack the living and leave an undercurrent of fear and foreboding. They attack most often at night, possibly to avoid being seen. There is a lot of speculation as to what type of entity dark figures are, and their space on my chart is reflective of my own personal experience.

My perception of poltergeists is different than most schooled and experienced in paranormal/supernatural studies. My chart omits much that I believe to be conjecture and, in fact, misassigned culpability where they are concerned, but includes some of the signs attributed to them for generations. While gifted in the art of sound, I don't believe they cause loud, house-trembling noise. I believe such is attributable to demons and evil spirits.

I don't adhere to the RSPK theory as being an alternative definition of a poltergeist, but something entirely different. However, there are many more experienced than myself who do, and I try to stay open-minded and give it space on my chart.

To many, dark figures and ghosts are one in the same. In that case, one must add all the signs designated as ghostly hauntings to dark figures as well. Poltergeists and demons are often considered to be one in the same. Again, if this is what you believe, your chart would differ significantly from mine. If you have more than one entity invading your space, which is often the case, things become even more confusing. Add this to the fact that various entities can feign each other, most especially evil spirits and demons, and it becomes an even more difficult process.

Skeptics will bring out the human factors involved, and this is always important to consider. For example, a puddle of water can be caused from any number of things. If you have a dog, cat, or children, the possibilities are endless. Generally, my puddles are caused by a wayward ice cube which has fallen from the chute of my icemaker. If it is an unusual distance from my refrigerator, perhaps I've unknowingly kicked it there. Did I get out of the shower in a hurry to answer the phone and forget to wipe up possible wet spots? So many possibilities. I have found refrigerator/freezers are filled with many odd sounds that could be mistook for other-world entities!

Also, many seasoned paranormal investigators and those trying to see things from a religious perspective see things differently, and, indeed, we all do. The biggest deterrent to coming to some kind of consensus in this disquisition often stems from a variance in semantics. In my experience, I don't think it matters. What matters is knowing the difference between good and evil. Intuition, the gift of the Holy Ghost, or if you want to see it in a more practical way, instinct, are our best guides to understanding or dealing with what is paranormal/supernatural. If it attacks you, physically harms you, and thrives on making you miserable and fearful, it is evil and needs to be eradicated from your life. If it is something or someone unknown but seems to mean you no harm, you may choose to let things be.

So, as diverse as hauntings are, I offer my final thoughts to summarize the anatomy of mine. It is based on information gathered, intuition, spiritual insight, and my own life experience. It is not set in stone, and opposing points of view are equally relevant.

The place it all started was in the Manchester house. There are many reasons to believe that house was haunted—in particular, the fact that my mother and grandmother experienced what they considered a haunting there as well. I believe what haunted that house was an ill-intentioned ghost along with some residual energy from the past.

Starting my life out in a haunted house gave me a predisposition to experiencing future hauntings. Although the common consensus in the spiritual community is that we are all born with the ability to experience other-world entities, it is possible that if we are subjected to such at an early age, it becomes more pronounced.

I'm not sure where the dark Victorian man came from. There is no doubt in my mind that I saw him because he appeared to me many times. He is a mystery to me in that he didn't attack me like the other two dark figures. Because of my experience with the Victorian, I cannot label all dark figures as demonic...at least in my world.

He was probably in my childhood home when we moved there...a permanent fixture of some sort from the past. My family didn't seem to be as vulnerable to the paranormal/supernatural realm as I was. To my knowledge, nobody saw him but me, and I never saw him anywhere but in that house. I have not seen many entities, but the ones I have seen with my naked eye have served to widen my curiosity and defy my doubts.

I have been diagnosed as having bipolar disorder, probably brought on by the PTSD (post-traumatic stress disorder) resulting from my childhood hauntings and the actions of my father. The initiation at which I remember both is about the same, about three years of age. Although a psychiatrist or mental therapist could possibly chalk up my unusual experiences as being psychological in nature, I tend to believe that having a mental illness and the environment that often leads up to it, can put us in a vulnerable situation when seen through the perception of that which is evil. I like to use a little tongue-in-cheek humor in describing my own situation as "bipolar with paranormal tendencies." However, I do believe there is an element of truth to it.

The circumstances of my joining the Mormon Church and marrying a staunch LDS man with a strong faith in God probably kept my paranormal/supernatural proclivities at bay for many years. When both were out of the picture, I became prey to the evil spirits and demonic influences that I attracted through my negativity and questionable behavior. They would have been free to cause a lot of the chaos that went on in my Broomfield home. I had no tools with which to fight them—no faith in God, and very little knowledge of the paranormal or supernatural. The demonic attacks, although infrequent, continue to this day...consider learning from my errors in judgment.

I'm not sure what precipitated the haunting I experienced in the Broomfield house. Once again, I believe something negative may have occurred on the property in the recent or distant past that made it susceptible. However, someone else for whom the unseen world is nothing more than a ridiculous notion could probably live there without incident. I was a good target and brought on much of the haunting myself by messing with things

I didn't fully understand. My "devil may care" attitude and leaving God out of my life was also conducive to the kind of haunting I experienced. It is possible that I am solely responsible for my experience and that the property is not a part of its anatomy.

The deafening, torturous, house-shaking noises I heard, along with the incessant loud knocking in threes and otherwise, I believe was demonic. The duct tape incident, given its timing, which involved my studying the demonic, along with the fear I felt as something dark loomed over me, was pure evil. The beastly chomping and lapping sounds, along with the three-claw scratches which appeared on my body a few times, were also of the devil. The tongue clicking, rabbit incident, and paralytic attacks along with the increased fear factor I would feel at times over lesser things, leads me to believe there was demonic activity in my house.

While evil spirits are able to attack in their own way and make similar noise, their methods pale in comparison to those of a demon. Although I felt anger from what I perceived as a ghost at times, it felt more like frustration and a need for attention along with occasional temper tantrums than scare tactics. Its antics didn't begin to compare to what I consider demonic. I could fight the "John" entity off...not so with the demonic attacks.

I had supposed this chapter would lead to the end of my book, i.e., a plethora of possibilities and conclusions gathered as a result of studying the anatomy of my haunting. Also, an acknowledgment that you, my readers, may very well come up with a different, but equally germane interpretation. However, this somewhat incredible though true tale didn't come to fruition until my spirit guides set me straight a few months ago. The anatomical depiction of my haunting was yet incomplete. What follows is as big a surprise to me as it may be for you.

To believe that the recent haunting I've experienced is in no way related to my father would be an extension of the denial I have carried on my shoulders for years. To say it was entirely psychological would be simplistic and only a partial truth. The abuses I received at the hands of my father have been instigators of stress and self-loathing and have given me a predisposition toward the negative side of life. However, there is so much more…

CHAPTER FIFTEEN

Father

In early January of 2016, as I was thumbing through some of my notes, I came across some meditative writing I had no recollection of, it reads: "My father... his innate misery, far worse than mine."

On February 5 of the same year, about 6:00 A.M., I was lying in bed awake and heard an angry male voice say, "Get over it!" The voice was audible, and I was taken aback by the clarity of what I heard.

As I lie there in awe, I thought, "I can do that, but I'm not going to forget the experience. I forget a lot of things; where I put stuff, names, birthdays, etc., but I remember much of what has shaped my life, be they good or bad times. That doesn't mean I'm consumed by it all. I believe I have learned to whittle those times down to learning experiences. The beneficial stuff I try to keep at the forefront of my mind..." Then I thought, "Who in the hell was that?!"

I don't generally share my dreams. However, I experienced one on February 21, 2016, that I feel is pertinent to this chapter. It is as follows:

My father was still around, and I was a teenager. We were talking, and it seemed as though I had initiated the conversation. He was doing some carpentry work in one of the bedrooms of my childhood home.

The next thing I remember is that we were both lying on the bed, located in the bedroom where he had been working. We were on our backs, fully clothed, looking up toward the ceiling as we spoke. At one point during our conversation, I noticed him move a bit farther away from me. I felt it was his way of making sure I didn't get any false notions about his intentions. He was talking about doing what he wanted to do with his life. I felt he was referring to leaving. I pointed out that I understood and that I was planning on leaving as well. It was a comfortable conversation given the circumstances, since it seemed that it was after my sister and I had shared "the awful truth" with my mother. Although I felt he was somewhat angry and I was a bit uneasy during our talk, as I got up to leave, he reached over and touched my arm as a show of appropriate, fatherly affection.

A week or two after this, I found more meditative writing I didn't recollect. I was going through a bunch of loose papers, notes, etc., in an effort to get rid of some of the unimportant stuff, when I came across this: "This dark and malevolent one you call your father will continue in his evil ways, and you shall be plagued by many masters of darkness and deceit; 'tis your lot little one, and so it shall be." This was written in August of 2015. How could I have missed it? I obviously need to pay more attention to my writings. Maybe I read it and went into denial mode.

I've thought a lot about the term "little one." Although I am short in stature, when I read the above words, I felt an undercurrent of condescension and mockery in reference to my perceived naivety at not being aware of this "most obvious" bit of information. In my mind, I perceived it followed by fiendish laughter. Although I generally take information put out by evil entities with a grain of salt…this would be an exception. In retrospect, this bit of evil-intentioned drivel is only partially true.

I had felt so safe in my father's arms as he carried me through that blustery, inclement night into the shelter of the Manchester house so long ago. There were two occurrences therein that would shape my life in ways I could never have imagined…i.e., my first encounter with the paranormal and the initiation of the inappropriate, abusive relationship I had with my father.

The latter part of October 2016, unprovoked and without warning, I received a message from my spirit guides that literally stopped me dead in my tracks. I was told that until I took care of the unfinished business I had with my father, there was nothing more they could do for me. It was the most discernible, telepathic message I had ever received from them. In all fairness to my last two psychotherapists, they tried in every way they could to convince me of the same thing. Fortunately, they didn't drop me like a hot potato as I felt my spirit guides did when I assured them I had already done what they were asking of me. I suddenly felt all alone in a foreign land. My mind went back to a strange set of circumstances which occurred in 2006:

As I sat in the family room of my mother's home with her and my siblings, my daughter called to give me the unexpected revelation that my father had passed away in 2000. My eldest son had decided to get some genealogy done, and the genealogist involved had been able to gather that information. The situation of our all being together at the time of this announcement was uncanny. My brother and I, no longer Washingtonians, had joined the rest of the family due to a health scare involving my mother.

We all sat there with what seemed to be the same reaction…complete indifference to a moment that one would think should be met with some kind of emotion. Our father had been gone from our lives for a majority of our years at that point. My sister was a bit of an exception but obviously hadn't heard from him for several years. She had mentioned to me, on more than one occasion, that he had inquired as to why he hadn't heard from me in his letters to her. His relayed inquiries had fallen on deaf ears.

It was after my mother's passing in 2008 that I finally grieved his death. I was in the basement of my Broomfield home and was putting some of my mother's memoirs away in a dresser I was storing down there. I noticed the box where I keep some photos, cassette tapes, and letters from my father. I opened it up, and the tears started to flow.

I recalled the kind things he had done and spoke to him aloud. I wish I could remember what all I said, but I don't, just that it was spoken in the spirit of love and forgiveness. At the time, I felt this was therapeutic and something my last psychotherapist would be pleased with. He was but continued to voice his opinion throughout the rest of my time with him that I wasn't finished; in retrospect, he was very insightful.

Finally, with no idea where to go with the last bit of information received from my spirit guides, I pleaded for their help. It didn't come immediately, but within a few days I had received two messages from them. The first one, "You turned your back on your father...how does that feel?" After mulling that around in my mind for a few days, another one, "Could it be that you owe him an apology?"

Then, a few days after that, I was looking for something completely unrelated to any of this and found a letter I had received from him shortly after my parents' divorce and his move to Guam...probably written between 1969 and 1970. How it had escaped from its box and found its way from a downstairs bedroom closet and up into my master bedroom is a mystery. It was a kind letter, as most of our communication back and forth was. It was obvious that he had wanted to stay in touch and consisted of a descriptive narrative of his new home and job along with some advice about my needing to broaden my horizons a bit. My life was completely immersed in the Mormon Church, and he was concerned that I was missing out on other valuable, unrelated experiences this world has to offer. I didn't listen to him then, but he had been right. My heart dropped. How could I have been so cruel and thoughtless? He had started showing a better side immediately following my parent's separation. I had taken a weak moment and some ill-chosen words and cut him out of my life.

Turning my back on him had never felt good. Although I rationalized it, telling myself it wasn't just about me but for my family that I needed to eradicate him from my life, it wasn't completely true. Yes, it made sense, but the truth is that I was just too tired and busy to deal with the things I should have dealt with where he was concerned. It was after a visit from his new home in Palau that I recalled how taxing being around him could be:

The visit was in 1973. My daughter would have been close to three, and my first-born son was still getting around on all fours—not much over a year old. My father would greet me in the kitchen as soon as I was up feeding my son breakfast and talk almost non-stop for the rest of the day. Leaving either of my children alone with him was out of the question for obvious reasons. I would be so worn down by the end of the day, one would think I would collapse into a coma at its end…but that wouldn't happen. I spent my nights worrying about what the next day would bring.

Although my father didn't seem to realize, or stop to think about the fact, that my husband might be aware of the incestuous nature of our past relationship, he did know, and that caused me great anxiety. Needless to say, he was one of the most despicable of humankind where my highly religious Mormon spouse was concerned and in fact had committed an unpardonable sin in both of our minds and according to Mormon doctrine. Although my husband wasn't around for most of his visit, I worried about what could happen between the two of them. To my husband's credit, he showed a lot of restraint.

By the time my father left, after only a few days, I was thoroughly exhausted. He had been on his best behavior the entire time, but he was too much for me. I never wanted to be around him again. I spent my days before and after our visit not only caring for my own children but babysitting as well, and I was always inundated with church work. I was overwhelmed and worried that he might come back again someday; it became one of my worst nightmares.

I heard from him shortly after he left, as I had before. He would overpay me to send him various things from the states that he couldn't get on the beautiful, although remote island of Palau. It wasn't long after his visit that he asked me to ship him an exhaust system for his Travelall…his mode of transportation.

I had always done what my father asked of me, but I couldn't figure out how to do this and was already overwhelmed by my responsibilities at home. Wracked with guilt, I finally sent him an apologetic reply to his request a few months later, telling him I didn't have the "know how" to do what he had asked. What followed was a cassette tape which included a few expletives regarding my family and myself, and the statement, "I don't care if I ever hear from any of you again." He seemed intoxicated on the tape, and I felt he didn't mean what he had said. However, I saw it as my way out. He never heard from me again.

When I finished my little memorial speech in the basement of my Broomfield home, I felt I had accomplished something great…but it was all about me. At that point in time, I had not yet accepted the odd happenings in my home as paranormal. Even after the haunting became undeniable to me, I didn't think of my father as being a part of it. Hind sight is sometimes 20/20…

It wasn't until my spirit guides raised my antenna a bit in October of 2016 that I even surmised that he might have had anything to do with the Broomfield haunting. I can't express with mere words the difference that bit of information and my ensuing actions have had on my life. I never anticipated when I started writing this book that this would be a part of its conclusion. There is far more room in my heart for love, acceptance, and understanding for others because of this revelation.

As far as the Broomfield haunting being attributed in part to my father, I can't ignore some of the more obvious signs. For instance, his acts of cruelty toward the domesticated creatures in our childhood home, namely, dogs and cats. Something as benign as barking too much or making a mess in the house was grounds for kicking, beating, and locking up our canine pets, sometimes for days. He once killed a pet cat for jumping on the kitchen counter and feasting on a steak. Fast forward to my Broomfield home: The racket picked up on my camcorder coming from the garage of a dog being agitated by banging on the garage door and other racket. It seemed that one of the "garage dwellers" received some pleasure from afflicting such agitation.

My house guest, who tripped in the dark on the large area rug that had been pulled back as if to cause an accident. This man was not someone my father would have been drawn to. Neither of us turned the rug back, and it seems to me, given the act's repetition after the fact, there is little doubt that it was a deliberate stunt brought on by one of my unseen housemates. It was a large (approximately 5' × 8') decorative, stiff rug. No one else had been in the house but the two of us the entire day. I can see my father doing something like that in life. He would have been the same hot-tempered, somewhat opinionated guy—just wandering the earth without a body.

The long, tacky line of unexplained goo underneath the three-framed chain of pictures that I excluded him from. Cleaning products and prep work done with a new paint job wouldn't budge or cover it. The same pewter frame grouping is now hanging downstairs in the family room of my new home. No gooey substance is leaking from it there. I have the missing picture of my father and I in an upright frame included with other family pictures in my bedroom. It was with a certain amount of vengeance that I chose to leave him out back then. That vengeance no longer exists.

As an earthbound spirit haunting my home, I believe he would have been privy to conversations about the abuse he wielded in my childhood. I spoke about him on the phone in not so complimentary terms frequently with my three confidants, i.e., my daughter, sister, and childhood friend. This was not an uncommon topic of conversation. I was in therapy, and this subject, although given a roll of the eyes by me, was something my therapist brought up frequently and wanted to pursue.

The impact of my father's actions and resulting influence on my life has been overwhelming, and I spoke of him with a certain amount of anger and hate. I cannot imagine being him and hearing this kind of demeaning talk with no ability to defend, question, or even apologize for his actions. Being an earthbound spirit has got to be its own form of hell.

The phone conversations that were interrupted by static, etc., were during times I would be carrying on a conversation with one of my confidants, and it could have been when we were conversing about him. I didn't take notice of what the interrupted conversations consisted of, since I was oblivious to the idea of my father being part of the haunting at the time.

He also knew a lot about electricity and plumbing, in addition to carpentry. He could very well have been one of the culprits manipulating both while I was in the Broomfield home. Another telling indication of his possible culpability in these feats is his conscience. Yes, he had one. When I wandered the house lamenting what it was going to cost me to get the electrical problems in my master bathroom fixed, that would have been something he could have identified with and decided to reverse.

His ability as a carpenter could have caused not just consternation over the work that was going on in the basement but the workmanship. He was a perfectionist in this area of his life and would not have been pleased with the way things were being done. His temper tantrums could have caused a lot of the noise throughout the house.

As much as I would like to overlook the butt slaps, I can't. Spanking was a very common form of punishment in my childhood as it was for most children in those days. Perhaps it was his way of trying to make himself known, or perhaps he felt I needed a good spanking. The whistling I often heard in the basement where I believe he spent a lot of his time could also have been indicative of my father.

More so, being a mouse in the corner, so to speak, he would now know that I was the tattletale, not my sister, who initiated telling my mother about the sexual abuse. After separating from my mother, he did many kind things for me that he didn't do for my siblings. He bought me a car, took me on a trip to San Francisco, and gave me small sums of money I didn't ask for. I visited him many times before he left the country. We never spoke about the sexual abuse. The five quotes from my spirit guides and others via meditative writing and telepathy, sounded a warning that I needed to make things right with my father, a quick review:

> "My father: His innate misery worse than mine." (found in my writings in January of 2016)
>
> "This dark and malevolent one you call your father will continue in his evil ways, and you shall be plagued by many masters of darkness and deceit; 'tis your lot, little one, and so

it shall be." (Written in August of 2015, this bit of tripe showed up shortly after the above.)

I received the ultimatum from my guides in October of 2016, telling me I needed to take care of the unfinished business I had with my father. Although received telepathically and not spoken aloud, it was too out of left field and plain to misunderstand. Then, two additional messages given when they answered my pleas for help:

"You turned your back on your father. How does that make you feel?" (received in November of 2016)

"Could it be that you owe him an apology?" (sometime after the above quote, also in November of 2016)

As much as I would like to, I can't leave out the audible voices I heard on 4/21/15, "You'll be hearing more" and on 2/5/16, "Get over it!"

If he followed me to the townhouse, that would stifle contact with my spirit guides. More than once, paranormal investigators brought up the idea of an attachment. Did I unwittingly invite my father back into my life when I mourned his death in the basement of my Broomfield home after my mother's passing? When I opened that virtual Pandora's Box of memories, audibly spoke to him, sobbing all the while, I may have done just that! Although I think it is possible that my former property already had a propensity for a haunting along with my life experience feeding it, my actions that day would have served to enhance it...a perfect storm so to speak. (A word to the wise: If you decide to mourn the death of a loved one with whom you have a rocky past, consider a graveside or other place OUTSIDE the perimeters of your primary residence. A secluded area on a beach or in a forest might be good!) He died in 2000, and I moved into my home in 2006. I can't pinpoint exactly when things started going awry, but I know it started shortly after I moved in and intensified with time. By the time I mourned his death, there was already unexplained activity in my home; it would have been difficult to recognize a newcomer.

I decided to write my father a letter and at some point read it to him. It took some time, but I wanted to get back on good terms with my spirit guides, and I truly wanted to make things right with him. What resulted was a type-written letter, approximately two and a half pages long. Not an easy feat because I felt it would be my final communication with him and didn't want to leave anything out. What resulted, in condensed form, is this:

My reiteration that I have forgiven him for what I perceived as abuse from him throughout my childhood...physically, mentally, and sexually. Also, my lament that he never owned up to any of it. I didn't pussy-foot around the sexual abuse but expressed the contempt and dread I experienced throughout my early years over such an odious act. How trying to deal with the guilt I carried as a child, feeling I was committing a carnal sin against my mother and God, sometimes seemed unbearable. Finally, the terrible guilt I felt when I finally told my mother the awful truth which led to their divorce.

I reminisced about a few of the thoughtful things he had done (in fact there were many) but said that regardless of the good he had done, there was always an undercurrent of fear where he was concerned. I mentioned some of the things he did that frightened not just me, but my brothers and sister as well.

I brought up his visit in my adulthood and took responsibility for never voicing that all I ever really wanted from him was that he own up to the sexual abuse he had inflicted on me in my youth. I admitted that it was counterproductive to want an admission, never express that to him, and then cut off our communication. In reality, I don't believe he ever understood the full impact and detrimental nature of his actions. He had been abused as a child as well.

I acknowledged wanting him out of my life and that I took full advantage of his alcohol-fueled words of dismissal where my family and I were concerned. I knew in my heart that he didn't mean what he had said and I never felt good about taking his words at face value. From a psychological standpoint, since I had denied any remorse for my actions from the time I took them until this communication, that was a big step for me. To apologize to him was an equally exhaling moment. I had never felt good about turning my back on him; I had been lying to myself and others about that for far too long.

I forgave him for whatever his part was in the Broomfield haunting and told him that I held no ire against him for anything in the past. My parting words, "I wish you the best, and if there is a light you can follow to a better place, I wish that for you. Whatever your future holds, I am bidding you goodbye and telling you that regardless of whether you stay in this world or go on, to let me be…you need to leave." I was sobbing at that point. The mutual love and forgiveness I felt was worth it all. My letter was read to him sometime in the early morning hours of December 18, 2016. The guilt I had carried on my shoulders for so long was gone, and I hope my actions helped my father on his way to something better.

To say that I have learned something about judgment and forgiveness through all of this would be an understatement. It has changed my life. I wasn't mistaken when I journaled that I felt there was something around me that could hear everything I said and often responded to it. I can't help but recall the admonition I was made aware of early in life, to never speak ill of the dead. Although this was in reference to speaking ill of a person in the immediate aftermath of their death, I would suggest that one might be careful how they speak of the dead for at least the duration of their mortal lives!

Along this same train of thought, I feel it necessary to mention that I believe with all my heart and mind that my father had nothing to do with the attacks I experienced during my haunting. I'm not denying his part in the haunting and that a lot of it was fueled by his anger, but he was not one of my attackers. The quote put out by the evil entity insinuating otherwise I believe is a lie as it pertains to him. However, I believe there could have been more than one evil spirit attacking me as suggested by the evil entity.

Our creator has given us all gifts of discernment. What is right for one person may not be the best choice for another. This includes choosing those people we hold close in our lives, those we prefer to keep at a distance, and those we need to avoid. Regardless of these choices, we don't have the right to judge anyone. I've learned that in the spiritual realm, there is love and hope for all…including my father, and that brings me solace.

CHAPTER SIXTEEN
Childhood Hauntings Revisited

The evil "cover-tugger," dark Victorian man, and poltergeist, like the more innocent visions of sugarplums, still dance in my head from time to time. I've learned through the years and from my repetition of their stories that they are not unique. My retelling of them has often brought wide-eyed wonderment and has prompted a few to relate their own stories.

In times like these when technology has become king and using our own minds is somewhat obsolete, stories like these often don't fly. Likewise, modern technology is now available that captures voices and figures and precipitates interaction between the living and the dead. I am grateful to live in an age where I am allowed the privilege of delving into the mysteries of life which have forced their way into mine.

A couple years ago, I sat down to write, and my pen and mind became influenced by something I can't explain. What transpired, unedited, follows:

"There's very little to be said about your frail sphere. The earth speakers, be they probers, naysayers, or seekers, are sending out warnings about its forthcoming demise. The slothful ways of its ungrateful primary inhabitants are causing havoc and untimely death, not only to themselves, but for the beasts that share their space. Large amounts of currency

159

exchange hands for the false promise of making things better. All is not lost yet, but it will be...there is no answer to the problems at hand...and what of being a part of it all anyway? There are the breakers and the fixers, both scrambling around like ants in a pile. It's how the primaries exist. The fixers must have breakers, else there would be no purpose in their life and no livelihood.

Oh, and the interminable contests! Be they between congregations, countries, or individuals, all is a pale attempt to be better than the rest or be right. Winners and losers all make money for their efforts...rejoice?! Monuments in their highest form are mere representations of one life or event meaning more than another. It's all meaningless, for in the end, I understand, it's really just about you and how you feel and what you do about all this meaningless chaos you live in. And that brings me to the greatest contest of them all: The one between congregations.

Ah, yes, the eternal search for the truth. The only real truth is that there is none. It is simply about forming your own interpretation of it. The wise searcher realizes this and becomes at peace with the information they gather. They realize that the quest is a continual search. There is no contest for them, only the desire to do their best with the thimble of information they have. The rest don't care about doing their best...it's all about that filthy lucre they preach against. Be they pious, warmongers, dictators or presidents, if they aren't stealing it, they're using it for their own glorification. They, like all of you, serve a purpose.

Being physical and spiritual at the same time is a dichotomy...why choose such an abhorrent course? The spirit bound in mortality, always trying to escape but never fully able until the end. Dropping from the sky from those ridiculous winged objects with cloth to save you as you fall. Ha!

I have only fallen once, or so I hear, from grace they say…oh dear! I stood there and watched as my comrades went one way or the other…which of my brothers do I follow? Freedom to make wrong choices and mortality? Freedom is not free but sees itself in flagrant, meaningless ways. There is no end to anything that lives; world without end, life without end. There is no death, but a continuance of grief, poverty and joy to all who pay as they live.

I have spent my existence watching, following, musing, and puzzling over humankind. In the end, I couldn't make a decision and ended up in this strange mid-place where time has no meaning, sleep is unneedful, and "feeling" is something I merely recognize. I know not the physical nor emotional turmoil; without empathy, that sensation is lost for me. I recognize it in humans but find it perplexing. My final words in the turmoil, 'Catch me before I flee from emancipation on my knees.' And here I am; nothing to most, but I am."

However you perceive the paranormal or supernatural, it IS. In order for there to be a phony poltergeist, there must first be a real one. There is a counterfeit for all entities, including the human race.

My sister, who has lived in Manchester for most of her life, called me a few months ago as I was contemplating how to end this book. She told me the Manchester house was being demolished. Another seemingly strange, well-placed chronological event to add to so many others. The houses around it are all still standing.

Although happiness has been somewhat elusive to me, it is my interest in this life that has kept me going. It's all coming together and making sense to me for the first time. I believe there's a reason for it all, and the only person to hold accountable for the emotional, mental, spiritual bumps and bruises I've succumbed to is myself.

When the Broomfield haunting is re-examined and its parts are somewhat demystified, I am where I started…with what I call a poltergeist. Not wanting to be mistook for anything else, this unseen anomaly gave me warning long ago. Call it what you will…a few rhythmic taps, subtle sounds once in a while, a few misplaced items, and some magic here and there…it brings a smile to this old woman's face. "Tis at its best when felt as a breeze…" just as I am. We are both affected by our surroundings, and it is up to me to keep the tone of my environment on a tight rein. Its craft, once again, to be a cautionary touch-tone, and a reminder that there is much more to this life than just what is seen.

And one last piece of poetry. To those left wandering this world who are no longer a part of it, my heart reaches out:

To the Lost

Fellow travelers, grieving sons,
Freaks of nature soon be done.

Leave the portal long behind;
There is no foothold, except in your mind.

Prove your span, envelop your claim,
Pass the rubble, release your pain.

It's all about a journey that never ends;
Advance your movement and pass the bend.

It all leads nowhere, or we find our way,
Don't give up, Spirit away!

My life so far has given me much to ponder, and although I have no conclusions to offer, my beliefs, no matter how bizarre they may seem, are not as important as the behavior they have incited. I believe this is true for all of humanity. This world is our proving ground; our mortality, the affliction that defines us.

For me, my haunting and efforts to understand it, regardless of opposing views, has given rise to a further understanding of what my personal journey in this world is about. Dissecting it and laying out its parts has been a labor of discovery.

There have been only a few in my life for whom my interests have seemed relevant; and in fact, voicing them has made for the solitary nature of my existence. It is my hope to find a receptive audience for whom my adventures and non-scientific anatomy of a haunting may be of interest.

Finding a stopping place has been the most difficult part of this book but has led me to conclude that it is always good to finish one's story before its end; or shall I say, the only way...